Changing The Way We Do Church

Changing The Way We Do Church

A PRACTICAL GUIDE FOR LEADING YOUR CHURCH THROUGH CHANGE

Dr. Vernon D. Shelton Sr.

Foreword By Rev. Dr. Jimmy C. Baldwin, Sr.

ISBN: 1546579060
ISBN 13: 9781546579069

This Book Is Dedicated to my Family and
The Church
I Have the Privilege of Pastoring

The Holy Trinity Baptist Church
Amityville, NY

Acknowledgements

§

I WOULD LIKE TO TAKE this time to thank my Lord and Savior Jesus Christ who has blessed me beyond measure. It is only by His grace and mercy that I am who I am, and have accomplished so many great things in my life and ministry.

I am always grateful for my wife, LaPrena Shelton for being my partner in life and ministry. I will never forget your continuous support and the many sacrifices you have made over the years. You are my special gift from God! I would also like to thank God for our children (Terrance, Monique, Myriah, Ayona, and DJ) who has sacrificed so much since I entered into ministry. I am forever grateful for my parents Marolyn Tucker, Vernon G. Shelton, and Lynn Saunders who always pushed me to pursue all my dreams and aspirations. Thanks for believing in me! I thank God for my grandmother Francis Berman for setting the spiritual foundation of our family. I thank God for my In-laws Mrs. Darlene, Micheal and Grandma Jackie for their love and support. I thank God for all of my siblings (Scooby, Tish, Darrin, Shaquan, Angie, Isha, Sid, Kurt, Charde and Shawniece. I thank God for my entire family who always support my ministry.

I thank God for my friends who are also like brothers, Ronald McNair, Keith Miller, Kenny Powell, Demitrius (Man) Holmes, Ronald Scribner, Greg (Honey) Cunningham, Troy Blackwell, and Corey Tyson.

I thank God for my pastor and father in ministry Dr. Anthony M. Chandler Sr., for being a great example for me to follow and developing in me a Spirit of Excellence. Words cannot express the impact you have made in my life and ministry.

I will never forget the church that gave me a chance to cut my pastoral teeth, the New Hope Christian Baptist Church, Baltimore, MD. Pastor Robin Turner my daughter in ministry, I am so proud of the great work you are doing at New Hope.

What can I say about my church family The Holy Trinity Baptist Church; I love you from the bottom of my heart. Thank you for taking care of my family. Thank you for trusting me to lead you outside of your comfort zone to a journey of faith. We have accomplished so many great things together, but the good news is we are not finish yet!

In Loving memory of a few members who have impacted my life and ministry in a major way before they went home to be with the Lord. They will never be forgotten. Mother Murlie Gatling, Mother Elnora Walker, Mother Bernice Daniels, Sister Florence Calloway, Deacon Henry Stewart, Deacon Willie McClurkin, Deacon Kenneth Bailey, Sister Sheila Vann, Brother Melvin Smith, Deaconess Bernice Porter, Sister Eva Lawhorne and Master BJ McArthur.

I thank God for my editorial staff, Shauwanda Altman, Angela Mac-Brown, and Jordan Stevenson. Thank you for your hard work and insight. I thank God for my Eastern Baptist Association Family. Special shout out to the Congress of Christian Education Family and Staff.

I thank God for my accountability partners and brothers in ministry, Dr. Sedgwick Easley, Rev. C. Omarr Evans, Dr. Lemuel Mobley, Rev. Evan Gray, Dr. Kevin Northam, Rev. Jeffery Thompson, Rev. Patrick Young, Rev. Donald Butler, Rev. Herman Washington, Dr. Daris Dixon-Clark, Rev. Gary Johnson, Dr. Larry Camp, Bishop Phillip Elliott, Rev. Christopher Howard, Rev. Stephen Lawrence and Dr. Alonzo Smith. I cannot forget my sister Rev. MarQuerita Story, one of God's greatest preachers!

I want to give a special thank you to my Moderator Rev. Gilbert Pickett Sr. for trusting me to serve as the Congress President and always looking out for me in ministry. I am forever grateful.

I want to thank Dr. Carl Washington Jr., Rev. Norman Coleman, Dr. Patricia Rickenbacker, Dr. Ronald Grant, and Dr. Elliott Cuff for enlarging my territory and allowing me to serve in our State and National Convention.

I want to thank my big brother Rev. Dr. Keith Hayward for always opening doors for me in ministry. Thank you for all of your support and encouragement. Although you are a Cowboys fan you are a blessing to my life!

Finally I want to thank every pastor, preacher, and lay member, who prayed for me and pushed me to be a better pastor and person. Thank you for all that you have deposited in my life.

Table of Contents

Foreword

§

EVERY PASTOR AND CHURCH LEADER should frequently ask and answer the question "how's business?" This is an important and necessary question for multiple reasons. The first reason is because of the significance of the Christian Church. The church matters. It is the most significant entity/institution on the planet. According to our Lord the church is the light of the world and the salt of the earth. In other words, without the church the world would be dark, rotten and tasteless. It can be said as the church goes so goes the world.

The second reason it is important to ask and answer the question "how's business" is because it forces the stewards of the Christian Church to clearly identify the mission she has been given by her Lord, and to make an assessment of her faithfulness to the assignment. After the Lord Jesus Christ was raised from the dead and before his ascension he met with his disciples and gave them the directives for the business they were to be engaged in. The disciples, as stewards of the church, had the responsibility of carrying out the mandate of the Master with the aid of the Holy Spirit. The question "how's business" can serve as a useful tool in getting those who lead the church in her endeavors to focus on the real/right business and seek ways to do the business better.

The third reason it is important to ask and answer the question "how's business" is because an honest answer will reveal the state of the Christian Church. To some, unfortunately, the state of the church is not deemed an important concern as it should be. Some might argue that because the Lord Jesus Christ made it clear that the church cannot be stopped there should be no reason to be concerned about the state of the church. In St Matthew 16 Jesus said to Peter and the other disciples "I will build my church and the gates of hell will never prevail against it". The Lord Jesus plainly states there is no force on the planet (political, social, economic, human or demonic) that can stop the church. However, it is also clear that all of those factors can and often affect the state of the church.

Personally, I believe the state of the church is extremely important. In Ephesians the Apostle Paul wrote God gave ministry gifts to the church for the purpose of building strong and mature believers who would do the work of the ministry. A healthy church is what God wants and uses to advance His goodwill in the earth. Yet there are forces that are warring against and threaten not the existence but the healthy state of the church. To protect the church against these attacks and attempts, the Holy Spirit warns of the potential danger to the church and informs the church on how to address that potential danger.

In this book Pastor Vernon Shelton shares his perspective on the state of the church and offers suggestions and recommendations on how we can do better in the business of spreading the gospel and making disciples. No other business in the world offers or can do what the church does.

Rev. Dr. Jimmy C. Baldwin, Sr., Pastor
Shiloh Christian Community Church,
Baltimore, Maryland

The Church Is In Trouble

The Church Is In Trouble

CODE RED, THE CHURCH IS IN TROUBLE! What's happening to the church? This is a question that has been asked by many believers over the last few years. I am not sure if you noticed, but something is going on with the church. In some places the church as we know it, has drifted into an unrecognizable state. The edifices are still the same, the names and locations remain; however, when you enter in, it no longer looks or feels like the church. I remember as a child growing up in Baltimore, Sunday was my favorite day of the week. Sunday was "church day," and we knew we would be there all day long. My neighbors, The Powells, would pile all of us up in that blue station wagon and take us to church. There we would stay from sun up to sun down. It was at church that we learned about God, Jesus Christ and the Holy Spirit. We learned the books of the bible and the basics of Christianity. Most of all, we learned the meaning and the reason for our salvation. Church was the place where we developed our spiritual foundation.

As I grew older, the church became that safe and comforting place. It was the place where I went to find comfort and guidance to deal with life's problems. It was the place I gained new family members outside of my biological family. Also, church was the place where I developed healthy and long-lasting relationships/friendships.

I remember how members showed genuine compassion and concern for whatever challenges I faced, without being judgmental. Thinking back on those times, I can honestly say the church helped me get through some of the most trying times of my life.

However, the church is not like it used to be. These days, you have to be careful about the relationships you form at church, because all churchgoers are not Christ-like. Some relationships you form at church can be the source of your greatest pain, or a distraction to your Christian walk. Therefore, be very careful with whom you connect with while trying to become a God-fearing disciple. Make sure you build healthy, spiritual relationships that will draw you nearer to God and encourage you to become a better person.

Furthermore, nowadays you also have to be careful about sharing your personal issues at church. There was a time when the church was set up to help you work through hardships. However, in this day and age you have to be very selective with whom you share your issues. Some people have given their life to Christ, joined a church and unfortunately developed a sudden case of amnesia. They have become very egotistical and judgmental, as if they have arrived and are sin free. But apparently they forgot the bible says in Romans 3:23 that, "all have sinned and fallen short of the glory of God." It also says in John 8:7, "Let he who is without sin throw the first stone." This literally means none of us are perfect, and because we are not perfect, we have no right to judge someone else for their sin. Judgement belongs to God. We are to encourage one another and build each other up 1Thessalonians 5:11.

CONGREGATIONS ARE DECLINING
What's happening to the church? Where is the zeal? There was a time when the church was filled with excited worshippers zealous

to hear the word of God. However, times have changed as it relates to committed worshippers. I do not know if you have noticed, but many congregations are declining. People just don't attend church the way they once did. Throughout the late 1980's and 1990's, churches were packed with parishioners of all ages. Many churches had to add additional worship services, while others had to build bigger sanctuaries to accommodate the large crowds. Back in those days, pastors did not have to beg or persuade members to attend weekday or afternoon services; whenever the doors of the church were opened, members showed up in great numbers. However, over the last fifteen years times have really changed. Many churches are no longer experiencing exponential growth in membership; they are actually experiencing a decrease and are fighting to hold onto the faithful few.

All congregations at some point will have to deal with a decrease in membership for various reasons. For example, we all must cope with the death of faithful members. In addition to death, members retire and relocate, get married and transfer their membership to fellowship with their spouse; the children grow older and matriculate to college and the list goes on and on. However, those are just a few reasons why our congregations decrease, but in most cases people are just not committed to the church like they were before. Church is no longer a priority in their lives. It is a sad reality, but in today's society the church has to compete for the time and attention of its' members, which has hurt many congregations.

There are many reasons why congregations are declining, and if these reasons go unnoticed or unaddressed, we will be left with a remnant. At some point we must address these issues and implement a plan to keep our members connected to God and the church. This is a clarion call to all churches and pastors; we must be vigilant and dutiful if our churches are to continuously grow.

Some Churches Are Struggling Financially

Another reason why some churches are in trouble is because they are struggling financially. Let's just deal with the elephant in the room and not beat around the bush; the money is not there, because people do not give the way they did before. Those faithful tithing members are few in number. Seniors are living on a fixed income, and a lot of the working class have so much debt that they are tossed between "two opinions;" whether to pay their tithes or their bills. Depending on where they are spiritually, in most cases their bills will get paid first and God will get what's left. It is unfortunate that we are living in a day and time where you have to almost beg people who say they love God, to give Him what He requires in His Word, and that is to, "Bring the whole tithe into the storehouse."- Malachi 3:10. If we love God, and believe what He says in His Word, no one should have to persuade us to be obedient in our giving. We should not have to be threatened with a "spiritual curse" to be motivated to give. The bible is clear, "God loves a cheerful giver - 2 Corinthians 8:1- 9:14. What most believers should understand is that giving is an act of worship and obedience to God! Therefore, the way we give should reflect our faith and our love for God.

Moreover, for some pastors, the church's finances are the main area of stress and concern. Many churches struggle week to week, and cannot afford to miss a Sunday. Winter and summer have proven to be tough seasons for churches who are struggling financially. This is because many members stay home at the thought of bad weather, and take off the summer for vacations. However, staying home because of bad weather and traveling during the summer is not the issue; the issue is when they return from their vacations their tithes and offering stay home or on the Island of Jamaica! Unfortunately, bills and expenses do not take off for the summer or even care if members stay home because of bad weather conditions; they still have to be paid. This can cause stress and financial challenges for pastors and trustee boards.

However, bad weather and summer vacations are not the only reason churches struggle financially; some churches struggle for many other reasons. For example, giving suffers in churches where there is no shared vision, when the trustees cannot be trusted, or when members feel the pastor has made poor financial decisions. When members feel that something underhanded or deceitful is being done with "church funds" they "protest with their pocketbooks;" meaning they withhold their money. On the other hand, if members feel their money will be used properly, they are more likely to be better stewards and support the church in all of its efforts. But whatever the case may be, the bottom line is still the same, many churches are struggling financially.

This problem has caused many challenges in staffing, worship services and building usage. Due to the decrease in revenue, churches had to revise their overall budget, cut salaries, lay-off employees, minimize building usage and find ways to bring in additional revenue. In some cases, the financial burden was so heavy that churches were forced to closed their doors and combine with another congregation. Other churches have rented space to outside agencies as a source of income. Unfortunately, the days of surviving solely off of tithes and offerings are over for some congregations. At least, until we change the way we do church!

Instead of Changing the World, Some Churches Are Becoming Like the World

The church is in trouble because in some cases it is hard to tell the difference between a church and a social club. Moreover, many churches have lost their identity trying to attract a younger generation of nonbelievers. 2 Corinthians 6:17; tells us to "Come out from among them and be ye separate". The church should be the beacon light that the world sees and conforms to. The mission of the church is to change the world, not be like the world. When nonbelievers come to church they are looking for something different than what they are getting in the world. They want to feel different, they want to be treated different, and they want to be looked at in a different way than how they are looked at in the world. This means, we do not have to compromise or lower our standards just to reach a younger generation of nonbelievers.

In the last few years many churches have upgraded their facilities and incorporated technology, which in some cases is necessary, in order to stay relevant and effective in this day and time. Let me say this to some who have yet to come into the 21st century, technology and the use of social media is not the devil. People do devilish things with technology and social media, but it in and of itself is not the devil. It can and has been a blessing to so many churches. The use of websites, email and Facebook, just to name a few, have saved thousands of dollars on postage, as well as expediting our form of communication. It has also enhanced the way we promote church events and announcements. Thank God for technology!

Moreover, the use of technology and social media can enhance your worship experience, but it should never take away from the authentic feeling of worship. There is nothing wrong with adding technology and other things to enrich the worship experience, such as screens, special lighting, and electronic giving, but whatever you add to the sanctuary should not take away the sanctity of being at church. The church should never try to be so relevant to the culture that it neglect its foundation, which is Christ! When you leave church you want to feel that you have been in the presence of God, not at a Broadway production, or at a rock band concert because the musicians blew you out of the building. Therefore, when incorporating things to enhance and enrich the worship service, be mindful not to eliminate the sanctity of worship.

Furthermore, in an attempt to attract and entertain nonbelievers, many churches have eliminated all of its traditional practices and traditional methods of worship. For example, many churches have eliminated Sunday school and bible study, and they focus only on the morning worship service. They no longer sing hymns or traditional gospel music which is foundational for the church; they only sing the new contemporary music. I personally like (some) of the new contemporary gospel music. However, I do not think it should replace traditional gospel music. Every church should have a balance of both traditional and contemporary gospel music to meet the needs and desires of everyone in the worship experience. I have always felt that you do not have to eliminate one in order to incorporate the other. The main factor when selecting music for your worship experience should be the message behind the music, not just the tempo or beat. Here is the bottom line, the hymns still work and some contemporary music can get the job done, as well. Therefore, it's important to find a balance in the selection of music to meet the needs of the entire congregation.

THE NEW NORMAL

One of the most recent challenges the church is facing is how to deal with the "New Normal." The things which used to be considered wrong and ungodly, especially for the church, have become normal in society. For instance, the church now has to deal with the legalization of same sex marriage. How does the church uphold its position and convictions of biblical marriage when the country has redefined marriage in a way that contradicts God's Word? At the same time, how does the church minister to those who struggle with their sexual orientation?

For many pastors, this has not been a major issue as of yet. However, what happens when two of your faithful tithe-paying same sex members decide they want to be married in their church? How do you handle this new normal, but at the same time uphold God's standard of marriage? These are challenges we all will have to face if we have not dealt with them already; and if we are not ready we can possibly handle it the wrong way.

WAKE UP, WE ARE DRIFTING. IT'S TIME TO CHANGE THE WAY WE DO CHURCH.

There are many challenges facing the church, however, one of the most critical problems is that many churches are asleep behind the wheel and do not realize they have a problem. Attendance has fallen off, finances have decreased, millennials are missing, and the church no longer looks or feels like church. Everything around us is changing daily, but many congregations are still operating the way they always have, and have not recognized the shift which has taken place. This is a "Code Red" for the church because we are drifting to a place of complacency and irrelevance in the minds of some people. It is time to wake up and realize that a shift that has taken place; and if we desire to get back on track, "We Must Change the Way We Do Church!"

This book is designed to offer some practical and biblical insight on how we can change the way we do church. However, if nothing in your church has changed and you are comfortable with its future, there is nothing you need to do. On the other hand, if you are ready to maximize your ministry and meet the needs of your congregation and community in this new season of change, keep reading!!!!!

CHAPTER ONE

Change Is Not A Bad Word

Change Is Not a Bad Word

"And no one pours new wine into old wineskins."

—MARK 2:22

WHETHER WE REALIZE IT OR not, everything in life is changing. Our bodies are changing, our families and friends are changing, our communities are changing, and even the church is changing. Some people may not recognize it or do not want to recognize it, but the world in which we live is changing. While change is difficult and sometimes frustrating, change is inevitable and essential for growth. All growth encompasses some form or type of change. However, change is not the problem, it's natural. People resisting change is the problem. One of the things I have learned as a pastor and a supervisor in the work field is that everybody does not like change. Everyone does not deal with change in a positive and Christ-like way, for various reasons. In some cases the change could benefit the individual, but they will still fight it, all because they have a negative perception of change.

This is really true in the church. You want to see some Holy Ghost filled, fire baptized saints act up, just start making changes in the church. Change can cause people to act contrary to their Christ-like character. In my opinion, people do not mind change in some areas of their lives, they just do not want a lot of change in the church. For example, every time a new iPhone or Android comes out they change their phones. When the flat screens and smart TVs came out, they got rid of the ones where you had to turn the channel using the knob. When Facebook, Twitter, Instagram, and Snapchat came out, they changed and stopped using My Space. We make changes all the time as we go through life, but when change takes place in the church it becomes a problem for some people. But just like we make certain changes to enhance the quality of our lives, we also have to make some changes to enhance the quality of our worship and productivity as a church.

Therefore, as leaders we must find ways to effectively teach the need for change, and strategically lead our congregations through the process of change. This is important because one of the main reasons people fight against change is because they do not understand the need to change. Oftentimes when Jesus taught a lesson He used parables and illustrations. For example, in Mark 2:18-22 when talking about change, Jesus told the people that you don't put a new patch on an old garment and you don't put new wine into an old wineskin. He wanted them to understand that if you put a new patch on an old garment, when the new patch shrinks due to washing, it will tear away from the older garment, making the tear worse. Similarly, new wine needs a new wineskin because as the new wine expands during the fermentation process, it stretches the wineskin. An old wineskin will burst under the pressure of new wine. Jesus was trying to illustrate that following Him requires change and you can't mix old religious rituals with new faith in Jesus. The Pharisees resisted this change Jesus was teaching because they were consumed with their own self-righteousness, and faith in Jesus could not be combined with self-righteous rituals.

Another reason people resist change is because they do not see the benefit in it. So, as leaders we have to help people understand not only what we are changing, but why we are changing. To effectively help people understand and accept change we have to first comprehend why people resist change. There are many different reasons why people reject or resist change, but I want to share a few that I found in the article, "Ten Reasons Why People Resist Change," written by Rosabeth Moss Kanter. In this article, Kanter says, people resist change because:

1) Change interferes with autonomy and can make people feel that they've lost control over their territory.

2) People will often prefer to remain mired in misery than to head toward an unknown.

3) Decisions imposed on people suddenly, with no time to get used to the idea or prepare for the consequences, are generally resisted. It's always easier to say No than to say Yes.

4) We are creatures of habit. Routines become automatic, but change jolts us into consciousness, sometimes in uncomfortable ways. Too many differences can be distracting or confusing.

5) By definition, change is a departure from the past. Those people associated with the last version — the one that didn't work, or the one that's being superseded — are likely to be defensive about it. When change involves a big shift of strategic direction, the people responsible for the previous direction dread the perception that they must have been wrong.

6) Concerns about competence. Can I do it? Change is resisted when it makes people feel stupid. They might express skepticism about whether the new software version will work or whether digital journalism is really an improvement, but down deep they are worried that their skills will be obsolete.

7) More work. Here is a universal challenge. Change is indeed more work. Those closest to the change in terms of designing and testing it are often overloaded, in part because of the inevitable unanticipated glitches in the middle of change, per "Kanter's Law" that "everything can look like a failure in the middle."

8) Ripple effects. Like tossing a pebble into a pond, change creates ripples, reaching distant spots in ever-widening circles. The ripples disrupt other departments, important customers, people well outside the venture or neighborhood, and they start to push back, rebelling against changes they had nothing to do with that interfere with their own activities.

9) Past resentments. The ghosts of the past are always lying in wait to haunt us. As long as everything is steady state, they remain out of sight. But the minute you need cooperation for something new or different, the ghosts spring into action. Old wounds reopen, historic resentments are remembered — sometimes going back many generations.

10) Change is resisted because it can hurt. When new technologies displace old ones, jobs can be lost; prices can be cut; investments can be wiped out. The best thing leaders can do when the changes they seek pose significant threat is to be honest, transparent, fast, and fair. Although leaders can't always make people feel comfortable with change, they can minimize discomfort. Diagnosing the sources of resistance

is the first step toward good solutions. And feedback from resistors can even be helpful in improving the process of gaining acceptance for change.

Moreover, our job as pastors, leaders and change agents is to help those who will be affected by the change, see the benefit and the need of it. We also have to get people to understand that change is not a bad word. Change can save lives, as well as rescue a dying church or ministry. A lot of people have problems with the word change, but we live in a world which changes every day. As previously mentioned, we as a people make changes all the time. For example, when a person has issues with their health, weight, blood pressure, sugar or cholesterol, one of the first things they have to do, if they want to live, is change their diet. When a relationship has become toxic or detrimental to a person's emotional well-being they make a change. When the remote is no longer working because of a dead battery, we change it. When the lightbulb blows out and it ceases to give light, we change it. When a tire blows on your car, you change it. Whenever something is malfunctioning or not getting the job done, we make changes so that we can keep living and enjoying the things of life. Therefore, when something is not working in the church, in order to get the desired results or the production needed, we have to make the necessary changes.

The bottom line is, change is natural; it's something we do all the time in life. Now here is the challenge, if this principle works in every area of life, what makes the church so different? As beneficial as change can be, why is it such a challenge in the church? In some congregations change is looked at as a bad word and it's met with forceful resistance. Only in the church will we know something is not working, or have not been effective, but will keep it because it's what has always been done. Or if that is not the case, only in the church will we keep people in positions that are not committed or getting the job done.

One of the reasons pastors face resistance when changing officers or ministry leaders is because some people think they are supposed to die in positions. The reason I know that to be true is because regardless of how long a person has been in position, when they are moved in order to give someone else a chance they get upset and sometimes leave the church. This does not apply to everyone. Some people understand the benefit of serving terms and changing leadership, but there are some people who get offended when they are changed from a position. The reason some people get upset is because they feel they are the only one who can get the job done. Even if they have not been effective in the position, some people feel a sense of entitlement to the position. It's a sad reality, but some people will allow a ministry to die as long as they are the leader or in charge. Unfortunately we are living in a time when some church–goers are more concerned about positions than they are about being productive.

Many churches are struggling and failing to get to the next level because they have people who have been in positions too long and one has to fight to make a change. I have noticed that when a sports team is constantly losing, the first thing people say is we need a new coach, or we need to change our players. When a business is not running smoothly or not producing the way it should, people say they need new management. However, there appears to be a double standard when it comes to the church, because when the church is not growing and the pastor makes changes in leadership or administration we often face resistance or pushback.

However, what some churches and believers have to understand is that there are times when change is necessary to get new results.

Sometimes change is necessary to preserve the life of a dying or un-productive ministry in the church. Change is paramount if we want to see souls saved and church growth. In Mark chapter 2:1-12 the bible says some men came bringing a paralyzed man on a mat trying to get him in the house to Jesus. However, they could not get him to Jesus the traditional way, and that is through the door, because the house was full. So they changed their approach and tore the roof off and lowered him through the ceiling. Sometimes it requires us to do something different in order to get people to Jesus, especially if the old way does not work.

The bottom line is this, change is not a bad word and it could make the difference between a flourishing church and a withering church. Furthermore, change could be the determining factor in helping someone give there life to Christ and join church. So before anyone fights against the change, they should first try to understand it, and see the benefit in it. The world is changing, our lives are changing, and our churches are changing, but we will be left behind unless we are also willing to change.

THE BENEFITS OF CHANGE

1) Change creates personal and spiritual growth.
2) Change prevents things from becoming stagnant and unfruitful.
3) Change ensures that bad situations do not last forever.
4) Change forces you out of your comfort zone.
5) Change creates new opportunities and experiences.
6) Change requires you to operate in faith.
7) Change can give new life and develop interest.

8) Change makes you flexible and adaptable.
9) Change leads to progress.
10) Change reminds you that anything is possible.

DISCUSSION QUESTIONS

1) What changes need to be made in your ministry to ensure continued growth?
2) Are you the only one who sees the need for change? If so, how will you get others to see the need for change also?
3) What will happen with your church if nothing changes?
4) What's preventing change from taking place in your church/ ministry? What steps will you take to help others get on board?
5) How can you get others to see that change is not a bad word?

Implementing Change

Implementing Change

CHANGE IS INEVITABLE! IN ORDER to grow a church and ministry in this day and time certain changes must occur. The way churches functioned twenty years ago may have been productive and effective in that era, but because so many things have changed over the years we cannot function the same way we did back then and expect to be relevant. Times have changed, people have changed and the way the church operates needs to also change, especially if we expect to grow and reach this generation. But what's important is how we go about implementing change. How a person implements change can make the difference between acceptance and resistance. I learned this lesson early on in my first pastorate, that implementing major changes in the church takes time, prayer and a lot of vision casting.

One of the biggest mistakes any leader/pastor can make is to implement major changes without properly showing the need or benefit for the change. Even if the change is one that will benefit the church or organization, without helping others see the need and benefit, people will fight against it or not support it. On the other hand, when the need for change is properly explained, and when members can clearly see the benefit of the change, it is welcomed without a great deal of resistance.

However, one thing we should all keep in mind is that you can do all the right things as it relates to explaining the vision and the need to change. You can clearly articulate the benefits of the change and how it will positively impact the church. But, you will always have a few individuals who will have a problem no matter what you say or do. These are the people who are never happy with anything, and will go against whatever you say. These people are so negative that they will disagree with you even if you repeat what they say. I call them "blessing blockers." "Blessing blockers" are people who do not like change or anything they are not in charge of. One of the main reasons they do not like change is because when change takes place they lose control and are no longer in charge. Also these individuals just have a spirit of defiance; they just like to fight against leadership and any change that hinders their perceived power.

The good thing is that "blessing blockers" are powerless against God's vision. Meaning, they can complain and fight all they want, but they cannot stop the move of God. They cannot block a vision that is inspired by God. Therefore, do not ever waste time entertaining 'blessing blockers," because they cannot hinder what God is doing in His church. They will cause problems and try to create doubt about the change or vision, but remember God has the last word. So stay focused and do what God has called you to do, even in the midst of "blessing blockers" and naysayers.

What I have discovered while leading God's people and implementing change is that oftentimes "blessing blockers" will fight the change, but when they see the benefit of the change they will try to act like they were always on board and even take credit for the change. In my first year of pastoring the Holy Trinity Baptist Church, God put on my heart to do some major renovations to our sanctuary. I am a firm believer that God's house must look its best at all times and we as believers should do whatever it takes to keep it looking good. Therefore, I met with our leaders and members about the vision to do some renovations to our church. Mainly, I wanted to get new carpet, take the old wood panel off the walls and paint the walls white. For the next few weeks I taught about the importance of taking care of God's house and the importance of appearance. I also taught that an old and raggedy church does not represent the God we serve, and it can be a turnoff to visitors and new converts. Thank God Holy Trinity was not in bad condition, but it could use a facelift.

Seeing the need to make some changes, I decided to cast vision through bible study and a few Sunday morning sermons, using the book of Haggai as my foundation scripture. I taught about the benefits of taking care of God's house, but I also talked about the danger of neglecting God's house; which is called the curse of futility (Haggai 1:5-9).

5 Now this is what the Lord Almighty says: "Give careful thought to your ways. 6 You have planted much, but harvested little. You eat, but never have enough. You drink, but never have your fill. You put on clothes, but are not warm. You earn wages, only to put them in a purse with holes in it." 7 This is what the Lord Almighty says: "Give careful thought to your ways. 8 Go up into the mountains and bring down timber and build my house, so that I may take pleasure in it and be honored," says the Lord. 9 "You expected much, but see, it turned out to be little. What you brought home, I blew away. Why?" declares the Lord Almighty. "Because of my house, which remains a ruin, while each of you is busy with your own house.

In addition to teaching the vision, when we would fellowship with other churches I would plant seeds by pointing out how good the church looked with white walls. Mostly everyone was on board with the vision of making our church look better. However, there were a few "blessing blockers" who had an issue with taking down the old wood panel that was already falling and fading in certain spots. For whatever reason, they were against getting rid of panel that had been on the walls since the church was built. The panel had no major spiritual significance; neither was it enhancing or edifying the worship experience. Furthermore, God was not going to deny us access into heaven because we took the old wooden panel off the walls. They were just against removing the old panels, even though it was going to improve the church's appearance. But thank God in the Baptist church the majority rule and the renovations were approved and completed. And I must say, it made a major difference in our sanctuary.

What was amazing is that some of the "blessing blockers" who fought against fixing up the church have since complimented the changes which have taken place. Some have probably even taken credit. Whether that is the case or not it does not matter, the only thing that matters is God's house is taken care of and positive change has taken place. Had we listened to those who did not want change and those who fought against change, we would have missed a great opportunity to enhance our appearance and invest in God's house. This project created excitement and a desire to fix other areas of our church, such as the fellowship hall, the annex, and installing a parking lot; all of which was paid for by fundraising and members' sacrificial giving. To God Be the Glory!

If you are planting a God-given vison or about to make some changes in your church, here are my suggestions: pray for direction on how to teach the change, take time to explain the benefits of the change, and do not allow "blessing blockers" to hinder the change. If God gave you the vision for the change, He will make it come to pass, and will give you the resources needed to bring it to pass.

THINGS TO REMEMBER WHEN IMPLEMENTING CHANGE

Everyone May Not Be Open To Change – Please do not think that because the vision sounds good to you that it is going to sound good to everyone else. Everybody will not see what you see and they may not think it is a good idea. However, when this happens do not get offended because they may not be fighting against your vision, it could be they need you to help them understand how it will benefit them and the church. Early on in my pastorate I used to think that when someone asked a question they were trying to be controversial, but I had to learn that not everyone is controversial, some people just want a better understanding, or they do not understand the need for change. So I have learned to be clear about articulating the vision and helping people get a better understanding. This does not mean that everyone will agree or get on board, but that is life and it is something we have to deal with in ministry. Not everyone will be open to change!

Change Does Not Happen Overnight – If you are implementing change in your church or casting a new vision you must have patience. It does not happen overnight, and sometimes it will take longer than we desire. One of the worst things you can do is get impatient and give up on the change. Be patient and keep pushing and eventually the change will take place. When people have been doing things a certain way for a long time, it takes time for them to adjust to something new or different. Therefore, we have to exercise a little patience, but at the same time keep the idea of change in front of the people and help them move toward where you are going instead of staying stuck where they used to be.

Get Your Leaders and Influential Members On Board First - One of the major mistakes a pastor/ministry leader can make is implementing change or a new vision without getting the other core leaders and influential members on board. I know you are excited about the vision, but do not allow your excitement to cause you to miss this important step. It is important to share the vision with key leaders and those influential members of your church before implementation. When they understand and have bought into the change/vision they will not only stand with you, they will help some of the naysayers understand it. This is exactly what Nehemiah did when he felt the call of God upon his life to go back to Jerusalem and rebuild the wall. Nehemiah 2:11-18 explains this principal:

> **11I went to Jerusalem, and after staying there three days 12I set out during the night with a few others. I had not told anyone what my God had put in my heart to do for Jerusalem. There were no mounts with me except the one I was riding on. 13By night I went out through the Valley Gate toward the Jackal Well and the Dung Gate, examining the walls of Jerusalem, which had been broken down, and its gates, which had been destroyed by fire. 14Then I moved on toward the Fountain Gate and the King's Pool, but there was not enough room for my mount to get through; 15so I went up the valley by night, examining the wall. Finally, I turned back and**

reentered through the Valley Gate. 16The officials did not know where I had gone or what I was doing, because as yet I had said nothing to the Jews or the priests or nobles or officials or any others who would be doing the work. 17Then I said to them, "You see the trouble we are in: Jerusalem lies in ruins, and its gates have been burned with fire. Come, let us rebuild the wall of Jerusalem, and we will no longer be in disgrace." 18I also told them about the gracious hand of my God on me and what the king had said to me. They replied, "Let us start rebuilding." So they began this good work.

Nehemiah understood that if he was going to accomplish this great work he needed the help of his leaders. This can be the determining factor of the success of your vision. Before you do anything, make sure the powerbrokers are on board; this will make your life and ministry easier.

Timing Is Everything – Timing is very important when implementing change. Some good visions have never manifested all because they were implemented at the wrong time. Major projects have fallen by the wayside because of bad timing. When God gives you an idea or a new vision it does not mean that it needs to be implemented the next day. Just because God gives you a vision to build a new sanctuary or a family life center does not mean go and take a loan that the church cannot afford. Vision takes time! It may take a year or so just to do the research and make the vision clear. However, God will reveal when it is time to move forward.

When it comes to making changes in the worship service or to the building, timing is also important. For the last few years when I made changes to our worship service I waited for the summer, when members expect something different. They knew that our summer schedule would be a little different from our normal order of worship. Therefore, whatever changes I wanted to make to our program or order of worship I would implement them over the summer. Doing it this way helped me alleviate a lot of the "why" questions. Also, when summer was over members would ask if we could continue with the new way instead of going back to the old order of worship. Of course I wanted to make the changes months ago, but timing is everything. Implementing change takes time, patience and wisdom, because not everyone is open to change.

Changing The Way We Worship

Changing the Way We Worship

HAVE YOU NOTICED THAT CHURCHES all across the country are not as full as they were years ago? For many churches, Sunday morning attendance has drastically declined; and in some states afternoon services are on life support or nonexistent. The bottom line is people just do not go to church like they used to. There are many factors which have caused this decline in attendance, but I only want to deal with one in this section and that is dry and disconnected worship services. Many worship services have become dry and lifeless, and no one wants to spend approximately two hours in a dry service. In addition to being dry, many worship services do not connect or engage the younger generations. The order of service is exactly the way it has been for the last 20 years. Some churches still have deacons who cannot sing leading devotions. Testimony service goes on forever because the same people are telling the same stories as if God has not done anything new. Choirs sing the same songs and there is nothing new or refreshing taking place. And they wonder why new people are not joining, and the youth and young adults are taking the first exit they can away from church.

There have been many books written trying to explain this great exodus. Conferences and seminars are taking place all across the country to figure out what's happening and what can be done. Maybe we have it all wrong; perhaps it's not an issue with people coming to church, it could be they are not going to some churches in particular. The reason there is a great exodus of millennials and young people from the church could be that they are tired of dry and disconnected worship services and they want to be spiritually refreshed and empowered. So they will go where they feel the spirit moving and they are connected in worship.

Over the years I have learned that seniors, millennials, and youth are different when it comes to their levels of tolerance and commitment to their church. Seniors are more likely to show up and stick with the church even if it is not spiritually uplifting. This is mainly because they love their church and they do not want to start over. However, millennials and young people are different. If they are not being fed spiritually, or getting anything out of the worship service they will either stop coming or go to another church that engages and uplifts them in worship.

This is why our worship services are so important. If our churches are going to continue to experience growth we must meet the spiritual needs of everyone, not just one particular group. This means you may have to update some things in your worship service. For example, instead of singing all hymns and anthems you may have to incorporate some of the newer gospel music into your Sunday service. Notice I put a strong emphasis on "some" because a lot of the newer contemporary music has a great sound, but it lacks biblical substance. On the flip side, do not be so contemporary that you no longer sing the hymns of the church. Some of the younger generation may not like hymns, but they still work and can create a good atmosphere for worship.

A healthy church is one with a balanced worship experience that meets the needs of everyone. One in which everybody, regardless of age, can get something out of it. So what that means is we have to evaluate our worship services to see if we have balance, and if we find that we are not meeting the needs of everyone, then we have to make the necessary adjustments and change the way we worship.

Stop here and ask yourself these questions!

1) Is everyone getting something out of our worship service or are we missing a particular group of believers? If yes, to part b, what has to be done to meet the spiritual needs of everyone?

2) Do the young people feel like they are an equal part of the worship experience, or are they only involved on youth emphasis Sunday?

3) Is your service so contemporary that the seniors no longer feel like they are in church?

4) Does everyone have the opportunity to participate/serve in your worship service or is it limited to certain individuals? For example, do lay members get a chance to read scripture, pray, do the welcome, etc. or is it only for a select group?

5) Is the preaching plain enough that children can understand it and profound enough that adults can be biblically and theologically inspired?

6) Do you need to invest in a children's church so that they can learn and have church that is relevant to their age, or do they sit in the sanctuary and play with their phone and IPad?

7) When planning your worship, do you have everyone in your congregation in mind? If No, it's time to rethink the way you worship?

MAKING ADJUSTMENTS

It is my opinion that we have to always find ways to keep our worship services spirit-filled, fresh, uplifting and engaging for everyone. Following a routine is good for structure, but there is nothing wrong with switching things up every now and then. One of the challenges in the church is some people do not like change, or should I say they do not like change in the church. When you make changes to the order of service for whatever reason some people think the spirit will not show up. These individuals give more power to the order of service in the program than they do the Holy Spirit. What they may not understand is the church will never experience the move of God when they restrict the Holy Spirit to the program. When it comes to our worship services remember God can change the program whenever He gets ready; it is His church. Therefore, we must be open to the move of God at all times and be ready because God may change the order of service.

Moreover, some of our worship services may need a few adjustments to meet the needs of everyone. But just like implementing a new vision you may have to help people understand how the adjustments will enhance the worship service. For example, in my church we no longer use the hymn books to sing our opening hymn; instead we print the words in the bulletin. Of course some wanted to know why we no longer use the hymn books. The hymn books are still in the back of the pews for those who prefer to use them, but printing the words in the bulletin made it easier for everyone. Also, we did not have enough hymn books in the sanctuary for everyone in attendance. To be fair we did not take away the old method of singing the hymn by removing the books completely, we just added a new method which we deemed easier; but whichever way a person prefers to sing the hymn it is available. A great lesson I learned in church is that doing something a new way does not mean you have to eliminate the old way. It just creates more opportunities to reach the same goal.

Technology

There are many things we can do to enhance our worship services, especially with the use of technology. Over the last few years technology has played an important role in our worship services. The way we communicate has definitely been enhanced through technology. There was a time when the only avenue to get information out was flyers and the morning church announcements. However, times have changed drastically with the use of websites, apps, Facebook, Twitter and other social media sites. This has made it possible to promote your events and get the information out cheaper and faster. In addition, we can now reach more people than ever before through the use of social media. We are living in a day when people do not call your church for information they just look at your website or Facebook page.

Unfortunately, some churches still have not tapped into these useful tools to help increase their witness. Yes, in the 21st century churches still do not have a website or a Facebook page or any type of social media. But they wonder why no millennials or Generation X's are attending or involved in the church. Social media may have some devilish things which take place on it, but technology is not the devil. It's a blessing if you utilize it correctly. We have saved money on stamps, envelops and flyers because of the use of social media and email. We are able to get information out to a wider audience and we are able to promote our ministry in a variety of ways. People have visited and ended up joining our church based on Facebook invitations and promotions. Social media can take your ministry publications to another level if you have the right people managing it.

Moreover, many churches have added TV screens and cameras in the sanctuary to enhance their worship experience. This can help with announcements, visual enhancements, words to songs, and bible verses just to name a few. Each church is different and what works for some may not work for others, but the bottom line is technology can provide aids to all of our services. However, just like anything else it is important to teach the congregation the benefit of what you are adding beforehand; this will hopefully eliminate some resistance. The reason I stated some resistance is because it does not matter what you do, some people are just not going to like it. And that is ok, but the overall impact will be beneficial to the congregation.

Music Ministry

Many churches struggle in the area of music. Could it be because a lot of individuals in our music ministry do not fully understand their purpose? The purpose of the music ministry is not to sing every Sunday, wear robes, and fight over who's going to lead the next song. The purpose of the music ministry is to share the gospel of Jesus Christ through song, encourage believers in their walk with Christ, lead the Congregation in worship and provide an avenue through which members may share their gift and be an integral part of the worship experience.

Here are a few tips to remember:

a) In order to be effective as a music ministry, each member must understand their purpose. Each member must know why they sing and to whom they are singing. In addition, each person must understand that the ministry is not about them, it's all about God! **God is the star, not you**!!!!!! Each member must have the spirit of John the Baptist. (Mark 1:7)

b)   Many choirs suffer and are full of unnecessary drama because of the spirit of competition. The spirit of competition kills unity (Gal. 6:4-5).

c)   The main ingredient to having an effective music ministry is everyone on the ministry must have a real relationship with God. The most important relationship is our relationship with God. Without being in relationship with God there is no worship. You don't become a worshipper by coming to church or joining a ministry; you become a worshipper when you have a real relationship with God.

d)   Real worship can only happen when we know God and respond to Him for whom He is and what He has done. A relationship with God is important because you can't authentically usher people into the presence of someone you don't know yourself. **You cannot lead worship if you are not a worshipper**!

e)   A relationship with God will help you fully understand what you're singing and why you're singing it! Some choirs struggle because they have too many members and not enough worshippers.

There is a major difference between members and worshippers! (Members entertain, worshippers edify and empower others. Members want to be seen; worshippers want the congregation to see Jesus. Members come when it's convenient, worshippers are committed). Are you a member, or a worshipper?

THE CHURCH IS NOT HOLLYWOOD (WE ARE CALLED TO BE SERVANTS NOT CELEBRITIES)

People don't come to church to be entertained, they come to be spiritually educated, empowered and edified! If the goal is to entertain the congregation all you have to do is sing well. However, if the goal of the music ministry is to create a spirit-filled atmosphere you have to do more than sing, you have to minister! There is a major difference between singing and ministering. Singing is the same as performing. Performing is for the pleasure and approval of the audience. Ministry is for the approval and glory of God! All members of the music ministry MUST be aware of this difference and make sure you are not performing when you are supposed to ministering.

NOTE:

You can sing with an attitude, but you can't minister with an attitude.

You can sing with a spirit of envy, but you can't minister being jealous.

You can sing while being arrogant, but you can't minister being arrogant.

You can sing with a life full of sin, but you can't minister without a repentant spirit.

What some music ministry members do not understand is that singing is based on your ability alone, but in order to minister to God's people, He has to empower you to do it. It is important to remember that God is not using vessels that want to be bigger than Him. If you want to be used by God you have to consecrate yourself and get rid of everything that's not of God before you stand in front of the people. (Exodus 3:1-11; Joshua 3:5).

The first step to being used by God is always personal cleansing. Without exception, when you find someone whom God is using in a great way, they've dealt with the personal sin in their lives before God. God uses small vessels, plain vessels, and even broken vessels. But He will not use a dirty vessel. *2 Timothy 2:21 says, "If you keep yourself pure, you will be a utensil God can use for his purpose. Your life will be clean, and you'll be ready for the Master to use you for every good work."*

PRACTICAL STEPS FOR BUILDING AN EFFECTIVE MUSIC MINISTRY
Everything Starts With Structure & Order! - 1 Corinthians 14:40 says, "Let all things be done decently and in order." God is a God of order; therefore, any ministry that represents Him must operate decently and in order. Without order all you have is a dysfunctional, non-effective ministry. In addition to order you need structure. Structure is necessary because a building without structure will collapse; a team without structure will fall apart; and a music ministry without structure will be characterized by last minute, thrown together music that doesn't add anything to the worship experience. Everything should start with order and structure, even rehearsals.

Much of the success of your music ministry will depend on what you do behind the scenes and in preparation for upcoming services and events. We must plan and prepare for worship and standing before God's people.

a) Make prayer a priority.
b) Do not wait until you get to choir rehearsal to select music.
c) Director and Musicians should know the music before teaching it.

d) Technology is your friend, use it. Listen to music ahead of time.

e) Talk with your pastor to see what theme or focus he/she has.

f) Promptness is a Must! **WE MUST ALWAYS START ON TIME!**

g) Presentation Matters! (2 Chronicles 9:1-9)

HOSPITALITY IN WORSHIP

Have you ever wondered how people feel when they visit your church? Do they feel welcomed or are they treated like an outsider who does not belong? The way we treat people when they visit our churches can determine whether they return or leave and never come back. A beautiful edifice is important, but a welcoming and loving environment is equally important. If our churches are going to continue to experience growth we must have a 5 Star spirit of hospitality. No one wants to join a coldhearted church with rude and unfriendly members who treat them like they do not belong. In addition, no one wants to be part of a church that is full of crews and cliques that treat new members like the enemy.

Hospitality is important to the growth of the ministry. Therefore, we have to ensure that the ushers or greeters on the doors have a nice demeanor and a pleasant spirit. We also have to ensure that our members are not rude to visitors because since they were late someone sat in their favorite seat. A smile and a pleasant spirit can go a long way, especially with visitors. In addition to ushers, some churches have incorporated hospitality ministries, whose sole purpose is to make guests feel welcomed. A hospitality ministry can be a great asset to every church because you will have pleasant, spirit-filled people on your front line making that first impression. Visitors may not remember the sermon or the singing, but they will never forget how the people made them feel.

GOALS OF HOSPITALITY MINISTRY IN WORSHIP

1) Make everyone feel welcome.
2) Maintain a presentation of excellence.
3) Be attentive at all times.
4) Maintain order in worship.
5) Minimize distractions during worship.
6) Always seek to speak an encouraging word to our guest.
7) Always focus on our strengths and seek to improve our weaknesses.
8) Be thoughtful and Christ-like in every relationship.
9) Always treat others as we hope to be treated.
10) Always seek the guidance of the Holy Spirit in every decision-making opportunity.

CHAPTER FOUR

Changing The Way We Give

Changing the Way We Give

FOR MANY CHURCHES, THE AREA of giving is one of its greatest challenges. It is clear that some believers are not as committed to God as they should be when it comes to their tithes and offerings. Unfortunately, a lot of churches have a low percentage of faithful tithers. Most people give something in the offering, but not everyone is giving what is required according to the biblical mandate found in (Leviticus 27:30-33; Numbers 18:21-28; Malachi 3:8-10.) This is one of the reasons why numerous churches are struggling financially. Some churches regrettably have to depend on the sale of chicken dinners and fundraising just to survive. I am by no means degrading any church who has to fundraise and do extra things to survive. Every church has to do whatever it takes to keep the lights on and pay bills, but that is not the way God designed or desires for His church to function. God's design is that tithes and offerings would take care of the expenses of the church. For that reason we have to constantly teach our congregations the biblical requirements of stewardship.

No More Excuses
One of the challenges countless churches face is that many of the members are not faithful in their giving. It has been said that some

members do not give because they do not fully understand the biblical principles of giving. In some cases that may be true, however, there are some who know about giving, but just refuse to give what they are supposed to. Or if that is not the case, they give but, their giving is not consistent. As frustrating as this may be, we cannot make someone give and be faithful in their stewardship. All we can do is teach them what God requires and pray that they will give out of their own convictions and understanding of God's word. Nonetheless, we can and should hold leaders to a standard. Faithful stewardship should be a mandate for all leaders. It may not seem fair to some people, but "To whom much is given, much is required." It is impossible to hold others to a standard that we as leaders are not upholding ourselves.

Over the years I have heard many reasons why people do not give in the church, and I must admit I have only found one that I agree with, and it is "I'm unemployed." I agree you cannot give money that you do not have. However, not having money does not mean you cannot contribute in other ways to your church. You can give your time and your talent. A person may not be able to give money to their church, but they can help their church save money. This can be done by cleaning the church, helping with the landscaping, and volunteering to do jobs that the church usually has to pay for. The bottom line is, not having an income does not mean you cannot contribute to your church.

Some of the other excuses I hear why people do not give are somewhat lame to me. For instance, I do not know where the money is going, I have other bills, or I do not like the pastor. I have even heard someone say "this church has enough money and they do not need mine." I'm sorry to disappoint some of you, but those are not acceptable reasons for not being faithful to what God requires in

His word! Your giving should not be based on your likes or dislikes; it should be based on your obediencc to God. We give because it's a requirement in the Word of God. But we also give because it is a privilege and an honor to give back a portion of that which God has given to us.

Furthermore, for those individuals who do not understand where the money goes, when you give your tithes and offerings you are not giving it to the pastor; you are giving it to God for the church. ***"Malachi says in chapter 3:10- bring the whole tithe into the store house, that there may be food in my house***. Money given to the church pays for salaries of church employees, utilities, building maintenance, materials for Sunday school literature, bulletins, cleaning supplies, missions, etc. For those who do not understand, it costs a lot of money to run a church on weekly basis. This is why when members do not give like they should the church struggles. If you are not tithing like you should let today be the start of your new beginning. Ask God to increase your faith so that you can walk in obedience to His word and become a faithful tither.

Moreover, I'm not sure if you have been taught this, but it is a dangerous thing to take care of your house and neglect God's house. This statement is made clear in Haggai chapter one. After God's people were delivered from their Babylonian captivity they went back home and they started rebuilding the temple. However, as soon as they started rebuilding the temple they were attacked by their enemy; this caused them to the stop working on the temple. But that was not the problem God had with His people. His problem was that 16 years had passed and they never went back to building the temple; instead they went and built themselves some nice paneled houses. God's house was lying in ruins, but they were living in nice gated communities. So Haggai came and gave them this word from the Lord. Haggai 1:2-6

> **2 This is what the Lord Almighty says: "These people say, 'The time has not yet come to rebuild the Lord's house.'" 3 Then the word of the Lord came through the prophet Haggai: 4 "Is it a time for you your-selves to be living in your paneled houses, while this house remains a ruin?"5 Now this is what the Lord Almighty says: "Give careful thought to your ways.**

Due to their neglect of God's house He punished them with the curse of futility. For those who are not familiar with the curse of futility, it is when God makes your labor and hard work pointless. This is exactly what God did to His children in Haggai 1:5-6. *"Now this is what the Lord Almighty says: Give careful thought to your ways. You have planted much, but have harvested little. You eat, but never have enough. You drink, but never have you fill. You put on clothes, but are not warm. You earn wages, only to put them in a purse with holes in it."* Also look what he says in **vs. 9-11** ~ *God said you expected much, but see it turned out to be little. What you brought home, I blew away. Why? Declares the Lord Almighty. Because My house, which remains a ruin, while each of you is busy with his own house. Therefore because of you the heavens withheld their dew and the earth its crops.*

Although they have worked hard planting their crops, they never enjoyed their harvest. So what that means is that whenever you neglect God, God will neglect you! Whenever you put your agenda ahead of God's agenda, no matter what you attempt, it will always come to nothing. When you fail to honor God, regardless of what you do, you will never be satisfied. You will never get ahead, never be on top, and never get out of a hole. That is the curse of futility. But because we are honoring God in our giving, we do not have to worry about the curse of futility. We have to get ready for the overflow of God's blessings.

Changing our Methods

One of the things we have recently added to our worship is multiple ways of giving (Online giving and credit card machine). Although some frown upon it, we have seen positive results and an increase in our giving. What we had to realize is that everyone does not carry checks, and some people just like to give electronically or use their card. We have added online giving through our website, and we also have a credit card machine for those who like to swipe. For those "Pharisees" who think that the only way you are supposed to give in church is by using an envelope, I'm sorry to tell you that day is over. Times have changed and if we do not want to be left behind or struggle financially, we have to adjust with the times. Online giving, credit card machines, and giving apps will not stop the Holy Spirit from showing up in your worship service. This may be hard for many people to accept, but all those new ways of giving serves the same purpose as the envelope. They are all methods of giving and one is not more spiritual than the other.

Therefore, whatever method(s) of giving that works for your church use it to your ability. However, one mistake which we can make is to add new methods of giving and take away the old ones. My recommendation is to add new ways of giving without eliminating the old way of giving (Envelope). This way you can meet the needs of the entire congregation and everybody can be happy. Well at least almost everybody!!!!!

THE BENEFIT OF ADDING VARIOUS METHODS OF GIVING:

1) It makes giving convenient.
2) Many people, especially millennials do not carry cash or write a lot of checks, but they will give online or by credit/debit card.
3) Members can still give while they are away on vacation.
4) If church is closed for bad weather members can give from home.
5) Non-members and visitors can sow into the ministry, especially on-line viewers.
6) It makes giving more secure.
7) Increases recurring giving.
8) People can give on days besides Sundays.

DISCUSSION QUESTIONS

1) Have we efficiently taught all of our members the biblical principles and requirements of giving?
2) What are the reasons some people do not give in our church, and what has to take place to change it?
3) What methods can we incorporate in our church to increase giving?
4) Do the members know where their money is going?
5) Are we doing what we said we were going to do with our money?

Changing The Way We Do Business

CHAPTER 5

Changing the Way
We Do Business

"Let All Things Be Done Decently and In Order"

- 1 Cor. 14:40

The Church Meeting

A FEW YEARS AFTER COLLEGE, I decided to turn my life around and get back into the church. I have to admit, when I first came back to church, it was an excitement that I never felt before. Church was uplifting, inspiring, and full of nice saved people; it was an overall fun place to be. Every Sunday after the benediction I left feeling great and eager to return the following week. It was not until I began to get a little more involved and started serving on ministries that I began to see things a little differently. I started noticing a difference in some people. Not everyone was as nice as they seemed to be on Sundays. People's attitude slightly changed toward me the more I got involved. Although church was fun at times, there was a lot going on behind the scenes. As a younger believer who really did not know all the ins and outs of church, I really did not know how to handle all the cliques and drama that was taking place within the church. But what almost caused me to leave church and never come back was my first "church meeting."

As a new member and a young believer I was confused and discouraged by the "church meeting." On that Sunday, the pastor encouraged everyone to come out so that we could discuss the business of the church; and the great things we had coming up for the New Year. I went to the meeting excited to hear what we were about to do in the upcoming year, and ways I could possibly get more involved with my church. But when I got to the meeting, we never talked about what we were planning to do for the year, nor did we discuss the great things we had already done. I sat there in amazement because all the people did was criticized the pastor and argue with each other. People who were usually quiet and pleasant during Sunday morning worship were yelling and acting like they wanted to fight. Members were disrespecting to the pastor and other leaders; and a few people even walked out the meeting. After an hour of sitting in chaos, I grabbed my coat and left, because I could no longer sit the midst of all that confusion. I also left because I did not feel that God was pleased with that meeting.

When I got home I told a friend of mine about the meeting and I vowed that I would never go to another church meeting. He responded by saying, "All church meetings are the same, because everyone does not come to handle the business of the church. Some people come to criticize, fuss and fight with one another." Due to that one bad experience, I did not attend another church meeting for many years. Although I was missing a lot of information about the church, I always gave an excuse why I could not attend. It was not until I became a licensed minister and a leader in the church that I started attending church meetings. Even then I felt the need to pray before the meeting, hoping nothing negative would take place.

For years I carried around a negative stigma about church meetings. Unfortunately, a lot of believers feel the same way. This is why many congregations have low attendance for their church meetings. For the most part people just want to know what is going on with the ministry, how much money we raised, how it was spent, and how much we have left. They really do not care about all the other stuff that has no major significance. No one wants to sit in a meeting and hear people argue for hours over titles, positions, colors, and who you like and dislike; especially new converts. None of that stuff helps us overcome our personal struggles and deal with the challenges we are facing in everyday life.

Moreover, I have discovered that some people come with the intent to cause confusion and discord in the meeting. When there is a problem, instead of addressing the issue when it happens, they will hold on to the problem for weeks, just so they can bring it up at the church meeting. These types of people do not want a solution to their problem, they just want an audience. They come to the meeting looking to cause divisiveness, and they will do whatever they can to get others to feel how they feel. We have to be careful about allowing these types of individuals to have a platform, because they can disrupt a productive and spirit-filled meeting with foolishness and unnecessary drama. They can make a good meeting turn bad.

The people I am referring to are not hard to point out; you can find them in every church. They are the ones who are always complaining. They disagree with everything. They always have something negative to say and never give any constructive feedback. They do not give much money and do not support any ministries, except the one they are a part of. They have a problem with everyone except the people in their crew. They do not feel that new people should be in leadership or working in any position, because they have not been a member long enough. They do not like any of the changes, and they wish the church could be like it was before the new pastor came. They are never happy, as if God has not done anything for them. They know the bible, but their lives do not reflect it. If you are reading this and you are saying, thank God I do not have people like that in my church," I would not celebrate too fast because they are a part of your church, they are just waiting for the right time to rise up and show their hand.

People like that are dangerous, especially in a church meeting because they will do anything to disrupt the whole meeting and create controversy. Those individuals say they love their church, but they will let the church suffer just to prove a point. This is why our meetings have to be spirit-led and moderated with complete order. I recommend you have a strong parliamentarian who can keep order, or eliminate people from going off the agenda. This will help you stay on topic and keep the meeting running smoothly. This does not mean that people cannot say what they mean, but they have to learn how to disagree without being disrespectful to each other.

If we are going to increase the attendance and get things accomplished, we have to change the bad label that is attached to church meetings. When talking about church meetings some people automatically think negative, and that has to change. The reason it has to change is because discussing the vision and the business of our church is very important to the ministries' growth. It enlightens members on where the church is headed; it shows strengths, weaknesses and the areas of improvement. It also provides an opportunity to show how God is blessing His church. Great things can take place at a church meeting if people would leave the negative spirits and personal agendas at home, and come ready to handle God's business. Whether the meeting is held in the sanctuary or the fellowship hall, it is still God's house, and people should not behave in ungodly ways in God's house.

In biblical antiquity you could not enter the holy place or the holy of holies with sin, a bad attitude or a goal to cause confusion. It was a sacred place, so sacred that the priest went in once a year, with a rope tied around his ankle just in case they had to pull him out after being struck dead because of entering God's presence with sin(Exodus 28:31-35). What we all must understand is that even at a church meeting there must be total reverence for God and His house. Therefore, when handling God's business we must conduct ourselves in a Christ-like manner at all times.

Changing the Label & Having Productive Meetings

1) Many pastors have changed the name from "church meeting" to business meeting, vision conference, etc. Sometimes changing the name helps change the identity. Do whatever works for your church, but we must change the negative label that's attached to the church meeting. It is our duty to cast vision and keep the people informed.

2) Start the meeting with worship to set a positive tone for the rest of the meeting.

3) Inform every one of the rules of the meeting, and help them to understand that the meeting will end if it gets out of control. In addition, help everyone understand that the church meeting is not the place to fuss and fight; it's the place to come together and strategize on how to take ministry to another level.

4) Change the setting. Have dinner or light refreshments before the meeting. This creates fellowship and relieves tension. If

that does not work you may need separate meetings, one for the financial report and the other for the ministry goals and expectations.

5) Have people put their concerns in writing and hand them in before the meeting. This can eliminate unexpected issues from popping up. It will also determine if they really want a solution or if they just want an audience to cause problems.

6) Commit to solving issues in another meeting with a smaller group (Pastor& Deacons) not in front of the congregation.

7) Stick to the written agenda!

8) Make sure all your core leaders are on the same page before the church meeting.

9) Handle all church business with integrity, and be transparent with the congregation. If they think you are hiding something then you will have a lot of questions and concerns.

10) Remember it is God's house and we have to conduct ourselves that way, even in a "church meeting."

STAFF AND VOLUNTEERS

A few years ago, while at the Hampton Ministers Conference, I went to lunch with a group of pastors after the morning session. During lunch we started discussing some of the challenges we were facing leading the church in the 21ˢᵗ century. Almost all of us admitted to seeing a decline in membership commitment and a drop in revenue. The conversation really became interesting when one of the pastors mentioned how he struggled to maintain his operating budget with thirty employees. We were trying to comprehend why he had so many employees, with less than one hundred active members. Some would consider a congregation with less than one hundred members to be a small church.

Moreover, he explained to us the reason the church had thirty employees was because the majority of his leaders and ministry workers were on payroll; such as his deacons, trustees, musical leaders, kitchen staff, janitors, parking lot attendants, and the list went on. The question which was raised at the table was why were all those individuals on payroll? He stated that having them on payroll gave him total control over what they did and how long they stayed in position! He also mentioned that because they were on payroll they did not give him any problems because they wanted their jobs. None of the other pastors at the table agreed with that model of ministry, but we all agreed that this model is probably the reason his church is struggling financially.

Unfortunately, we are living in a time when egos are driving churches in the ground and causing many of them to close their doors. For whatever reason, some pastors mistakenly think that having a large church staff makes you a "major" pastor, or somebody special in the kingdom. They think people are impressed based upon the number of individuals on your staff. But I have never seen someone give their life to Christ or join a church because they were impressed with the number of employees. Having a large staff on payroll is not something that we should brag about; especially if it is the reason the church is struggling financially. For the record, there are some churches that have the need for a large staff, but they also have the finances to support the staff.

In order to be effective and save the church some unnecessary stress, we have to learn how to live within our means. One of the greatest mistakes many churches make is trying to compete with the Mega Church. By that I mean trying to duplicate everything we see taking place in the mega church. There are some things we can learn from the mega church, but we have to understand that smaller churches do not have the same financial resources as some of the larger churches. Therefore, we should never put our churches in a financial hole trying to duplicate what we see taking place in the mega church, or any other church. Every church has to live within their financial limits and enjoy their uniqueness.

Furthermore, churches may not be able to hire as many full-time staff, or pay salaries like some of the larger churches, but that does not mean they cannot make ministry work and be effective as a church. When a church cannot hire a large staff they should not allow that to hinder the effectiveness of the ministry; they have to be creative and find other ways to make things work. Some may even consider the model that many catholic churches use. Numerous large catholic churches across the country do not have a lot of employees on staff; they use volunteers to fulfill certain roles. Due to the decline many churches are facing in membership and finances, this may be a direction they should consider. If this is the direction you take, it should be done prayerfully and with wisdom, because the use of volunteers can be a blessing, but it can also be burden for the church. Let's look at the pros and cons of using volunteers:

THE PROS OF USING VOLUNTEERS

1) We need them!
2) They help save money.
3) Gives members opportunities to work and utilize their spiritual gifts.
4) Gives members the opportunity to be a blessing to their church.

Cons of Using Church Volunteers

1) It is harder to hold them accountable.
2) They can leave or not show up at any time. Not always reliable.
3) May not always give 100%.

When using Church Volunteers:

1) Do not take them for granted.
2) Always have a backup plan. Remember anything can happen and they are volunteers.
3) Do not allow hired staff to belittle volunteers; everyone is important.
4) Thank your volunteers and show your appreciation as much as you can.

It is a fact that every church, whether large or small, utilizes volunteers in positions which are vital to the church. Without volunteers the church would be in trouble! The reason the church would be in trouble is because it is impossible to pay everyone for everything they do and maintain the budget. Although there are some people in the church who want to be paid for EVERYTHING, there are still some good stewards who are willing to do whatever it takes for their church to function. Thank God for those individuals who love God enough to utilize their gifts to be a blessing to the church and the body of Christ!

FUNDRAISING

I remember as a young man growing up I asked one of the leaders at the church what a building-fund was. She replied, "It is a fundraiser to keep the building running properly, and money to fix everything that is broken." I asked her what's being done with the money because I do not see anything being fixed, and why do you still give to the building fund, if they are not fixing the building? She said, "Because it's on the envelope." Unfortunately, a lot of people give money to building-funds because it's on the envelope, even though nothing is being done in the church. Some pastors and trustees may get mad at me for saying this, but I do not think anyone should give to a cause that's not being carried out. We cannot take people's money and not do what we promised. That's not operating with integrity.

When it comes to raising money, trust and integrity are important elements. Therefore, if the church is raising money for the building's renovation make sure the money is used on building renovations. Whatever purpose the money is being raised for, that is what the money should be used for. Now if something comes up and the money has to be used for another purpose, the church should be informed and kept abreast of the need to change. It may seem like a lot to do, but it builds trust with the congregation. People are willing to give when they know where their money is going and they feel you are doing the right thing. I have discovered this to be true in my own context.

In my first six years at Holy Trinity, we raised money for numerous renovation projects. The first project I proposed to the church was to install handicap accessible bathrooms on the upper level. We met and voted in a church meeting to go forward with the fundraising project. However, after doing some extensive research and getting professional estimates we realized that it was a bigger project than we initially thought. In order to install handicap accessible bathrooms on the upper level we would need to add on to our building and run water and sewer pipes from the street. Although, the idea was great, I knew we did not have the money to do that type of work at that point; and adding on to the building meant we would have to get permits and inspections for the rest of the building. So I chose to leave that project alone at that time. I'm sure pastors and trustees can understand why I decided to leave it alone.

Moreover, since we had already begun raising money, I went back to the church and explained the challenges we were facing and I suggested we pursue another project. We decided to use the money we had previously raised to renovate our sanctuary. Going back to the church and keeping them informed provided confidence and trust that we were doing the right thing with the money. It also made everyone feel a part of the process. This may seem like a lot to go through, but it proved to be beneficial because the members were willing to give and support the new project financially.

When a church is raising money for a specific project, keep in mind that things may change and plans may be altered. However, when that happens it is important to keep the congregation informed. If the vision changes and you decide to do something else with the money make sure the congregation is in agreement. Neglecting to keep people informed about changes to the original vision can cause doubt, and unnecessary confusion. It will also make people reluctant to give to anything else. This is why it is important to do what we say we are going to do with the money, and if anything changes keep the people informed.

HOW TO HANDLE SAME SEX MARRIAGE

One of the new challenges the church is facing is how to deal with same sex marriage. The law has been passed and same sex marriage is legal throughout the United States. This causes a serious challenge for those churches who upholds the biblical mandate of marriage between a male and female. Every church and every pastor needs to take this issue seriously because eventually you will be asked to perform a same sex wedding at your church. How will you respond? What do you have in place to defend your position, whatever that may be? The best advice I can give as it relates to how the church should deal with same sex marriage is "biblically and in love."

UNDERSTANDING THE CHALLENGE

According to Genesis 2:24, Matthew 19:4-6, Proverbs 18:22, marriage involves a man and a woman. The Hebrew word for "wife" is gender-specific; it cannot mean anything other than "a woman." There is no passage in Scripture that mentions a marriage involving anything other than a man and a woman. It is impossible for a family to form or human reproduction to take place asexually. Since God ordained sex to only take place between married couples, it follows that God's design is for the family unit to be formed when a man and woman come together in a sexual relationship and have children.

On June 26, 2015, the United States Supreme Court ruled 5-4 to redefine marriage. That decision declared that state-level bans on same-sex marriage are unconstitutional. The court ruled that the denial of marriage licenses to same-sex couples and the refusal to recognize those marriages performed in other jurisdictions violates the Due Process and the Equal Protection clauses of the Fourteenth Amendment of the United States Constitution. In so holding, the Supreme Court struck down the state constitutional amendments of many states which defined marriage as between one man and one woman. The decision redefines marriage for the entire country to include same-sex couples.

However, Supreme Court Justice Anthony Kennedy stated that: religions, and those who adhere to religious doctrines, may continue to advocate with utmost, sincere conviction that, by divine precepts, same-sex marriage should not be condoned. The First Amendment ensures that religious organizations and persons are given proper protection as they seek to teach the principles that are so fulfilling and so central to their lives and faiths, and to their own deep aspirations to continue the family structure they have long revered.

This statement is welcome to be sure. But the greatest threat for churches lies in the application of the court's decision to believers who live in jurisdictions covered by so-called "non-discrimination" laws and ordinances. Everywhere that marriage has been redefined in the last several years has seen an awakening of non-discrimination laws that prohibit discrimination in employment, housing, or places of public accommodation on the basis of sexual orientation or gender identity. In coming days, the threat from these non-discrimination laws will materialize in numerous ways as same-sex couples marry. But there are proactive steps churches can take to protect themselves.

What Should Churches Do?

1) Churches should update their statement of faith on the issues of marriage, human sexuality, and gender.

Now is the time for churches to maintain a clear witness to biblical truth about marriage, human sexuality and gender. Churches should update their statement of faith to include the congregation's belief on these issues. Doing it in the wake of the Supreme Court decision will not be viewed negatively by a court if a legal issue ever arises.

Instead, putting clarifying language in the statement of faith merely serves to codify a church's long-standing religious beliefs. Alliance Defending Freedom has sample language in its Protecting Your Ministry manual that provides a starting point. Clarifying the statement of faith can help a church in numerous ways. If your church has not done so already, now is the time.

2)   Update Bylaws

Have something in the church bylaws that state that your church will not perform same-sex weddings for members and non-members, but will conduct wedding ceremonies for one man and one woman as biologically designed by birth (to protect against having to perform "transgender weddings" between those identifying themselves as a man and a woman).

3)   Churches should ensure their facilities usage policies are revised to allow only uses consistent with the church's religious beliefs.

In the wake of the Supreme Court ruling, some churches may be approached by same-sex couples seeking to be married in the church facility. Churches should not feel as if they have to close their doors to the community just to prevent wedding ceremonies with which they disagree. Churches must continue to be a welcoming presence in the community and can do so through updating or revising their facility usage policy. The key point is to tie usage of the church's facility to the statement of faith and religious beliefs of the church. And then to make clear that uses inconsistent with those religious beliefs will not be allowed.

Sample:

WEDDING POLICY: (This is a sample of which can be added to your building usage policy).

At the **Name of Your Church**, we believe that it is our responsibility before God to help couples form Christian marriages, not just to perform Christian weddings. It is that understanding that shapes our wedding policy. Because God has ordained marriage and defined it as the covenant relationship between a man, a woman, and Himself, **Name of Church** will only recognize and host marriages between a biological man and a biological woman. Further, the pastor and ministerial staff, whether paid or unpaid, shall only participate in weddings and solemnize marriages between one man and one woman.

Biblical Foundation for Marriage:
Marriage is a Holy Covenant (Malachi 2:14 -15)

Marriage is the covenant act of a man and a woman uniting together as husband and wife Genesis 1:27; 2:22-25, which pictures the oneness of Christ with His church Ephesians 5:31-32. Marriage is for life Matthew 19:6

Alliance Defending Freedom has a sample facilities usage policy available in its Protecting Your Ministry manual.

The First Amendment states that Congress shall make no law respecting an establishment of religion, or prohibiting the free exercise thereof; or abridging the freedom of speech, or of the press; or the right of the people peaceably to assemble, and to petition the Government for a redress of grievances.

The First Amendment guarantees freedoms concerning religion, expression, assembly, and the right to petition. It forbids Congress from both promoting one religion over others and also restricting an individual's religious practices. It guarantees freedom of expression by prohibiting Congress from restricting the press or the rights of individuals to speak freely. It also guarantees the right of citizens to assemble peaceably and to petition their government.

The Fourteenth Amendment states that all persons born or naturalized in the United States and subject to the jurisdiction thereof, are citizens of the United States and of the State wherein they reside. No State shall make or enforce any law which shall abridge the privileges or immunities of citizens of the United States; nor shall any State deprive any person of life, liberty, or property, without due process of law; nor deny to any person within its jurisdiction the equal protection of the laws.

In closing, the way you handle your business will either help your church or cause major problems within the church. Integrity and transparency are important elements to have when conducting business and leading a church, especially when money is involved. Times have change and the way we handle the business affairs of the church has to also change, because the church cannot function the way it did years ago and expect to be productive.

Discussion Questions:

1) How can we improve the way we do business in the church?
2) Do the members have a negative view of the church meeting? If so, how can we change it?

3) Are the members confident with the way we handle capital campaigns and fundraising?
4) How can we utilize volunteers in our church?
5) Do you have a policy that clearly states your position on same sex marriage?

Changing The Way We Fellowship

Changing The Way We Fellowship

*Not forsaking the assembling of ourselves together, as
the manner of some is; but exhorting one another: and
so much the more, as ye see the day approaching.*

- HEBREWS 10:25

*"But if we walk in the light as He is in the light, we
have fellowship with one another, and the blood of
Jesus Christ His Son cleanses us from all sin."*

-1 JOHN 1:7

THE NEW TESTAMENT WORD FOR "fellowship," koinonia, expresses the idea of being together for mutual benefit. Fellowship helps believers express love to one another and it encourages good works. It also allows believers to come together for prayer, worship and spiritual edification. For the believer fellowship is an important mandate, and it is essential for our spiritual growth. However, for some people the word fellowship does not carry the same meaning it did once before. For instance, fellowships are not always based on mutual benefit. They are not always used for biblical and spiritual edification as originally intended; some fellowships are motivated by selfish ambitions, money and personal gain. When fellowships are not based on biblical principles no one really benefits spiritually.

When I served as a youth minister at the New Bethlehem Baptist Church in Baltimore I always looked forward to communion Sundays. Our communion was held every first Sunday at 3:30pm. The reason I enjoyed our communion service is because we always had a guest church come and fellowship with us. This is how I began to develop relationships with other youth ministers, and I got to know other ministers of the gospel. It was always a high time when other churches would come and join us for worship. However, over the years a lot of churches in Baltimore moved away from having a lot of evening services. For the most part Holy Communion and anniversaries were celebrated during the morning worship service.

In 2010, I relocated to Long Island New York and I discovered that the church culture is slightly different. Unlike Baltimore, a lot of the Baptist churches in New York love afternoon services. The afternoon service is a vital part of the church culture in my area. Now what's slightly different is that Holy Communion is usually served in the morning, but most anniversaries are celebrated in the afternoon. This allows a guest church to come and fellowship to help celebrate that particular ministry's anniversary. Depending on how far the church has to travel, dinner is usually served before the afternoon service. This allows the two churches to not only worship together, but to get to know each other through wholesome fellowship.

Another aspect of the afternoon service that is common in New York is that most fellowships are considered annual dates. Each year on that particular Sunday you are on the calendar for that church. This was a little different for me because I was taught to never assume a pastor is going to invite you back; you wait until you are invited. Although annual dates have been a part of the church's culture for years, it should always be evaluated and prayerfully considered. The reason why it should be evaluated annually and prayerfully considered is because it has pros and cons. The good things about having annual dates are it helps with planning your yearly calendar, and it builds relationships between the two churches. On the other hand, it can become unfruitful if the pastor/preacher looks at it as just another date on the calendar; and if that is how they see it then they will treat it as such.

It is my opinion that every engagement or fellowship should be approached with great humility and honor. We must fully understand that to be invited to preach in someone else's pulpit is an honor and privilege that should never be taken lightly. In addition, we must remember that we are not just fulfilling a calendar obligation, but we are on assignment by God to feed His people. Therefore, when we go to minister we should be prepared, prayed up and have labored over what God would have us to say. If the pastor has invited us to feed his flock, and the people have sacrificed their evening to be in church, the least we can do as preachers is give them a solid well prepared word from the Lord.

Unfortunately, this is not always the case. I have sat in afternoon services and watch preachers sit in the pulpit looking for something to say. There is a difference between God changing your word and you never taking time to seek God about a word. I found this to be very disturbing because it showed me that the preacher was not prepared to minister to my congregation. It also made me feel that the preacher did not take this engagement/assignment seriously. As pastors, we have to be careful how we allow preachers to treat our people. We would not allow someone to just whip something together to feed our children; neither should we allow someone whip sermons together to feed our congregations.

A senior pastor told me years ago that when I invite preachers to my church it should be because I trust their gift, and believe they will take the assignment seriously to edify or empower my people. He also told me to never invite preachers just because they can bring a nice check and have a good following. In addition, do not invite someone to preach at your church just because you want them to invite you to preach at their church. When you do that it is selfish and it is a disservice to your people. The quote I remember the most is "Never prostitute your pulpit to get blessed; if you take care of God's house and God's people He will take care of you and make sure you are blessed." These are words that has guided and challenged me at the same time. As they have challenged me I would also like to challenge every pastor who is reading this book. Let's make sure that when we invite preachers to come to our churches it's not only about money, but it's motivated by ministry.

Do They Want to Hear You Preach or Do They Want You to Fill Up the Pews/Plate

I may lose a few preaching engagements over this section, but that's ok. The year 2016 by far had to be one of the busiest years I have ever had for outside preaching engagements. When I looked at my itinerary, it gave me a good feeling to know that so many churches and pastors wanted me to come preach. However, my ego was immediately deflated when I started thinking that all of these engagements may not be about me preaching; some could be about filling up the pews and offering plates. My conscience started speaking to me saying, "What if the invitation is not really about you allowing God to minister through you the preached word; but instead, it's about the check and the people you bring with you? This statement first of all humbled me, but it also made me start wondering the motivation behind some of the invitations I was receiving.

Now let's be clear, when I'm invited to one of my brothers/sisters and close friends in ministry I want to bless them and take as many people as I can. That's just what we do for each other. On the other hand, when I do not have any type of relationship with the pastor or the church, no communication at all throughout the year and you invite me to come and all you are worried about who is coming with me, that's a problem. This type of invitation has money written all over it. That is also an invitation I will turn down.

It took me a few years to get here, but I'm finally at a place in my ministry that I do not have a problem saying I cannot accept and engagement. It is not based on arrogance or thinking I'm too good for a church, I just value my down time and my church family too much to accept every preaching engagement. I am prayerful where I go and where I take my church.

Every pastor should be careful and prayerful about every fellowship, because I have learned the hard way, that some pastors will take advantage of you and your church. If a pastor is inviting you to come preach for one of their anniversaries, it's not your job to fill up their church or make sure they meet their budget. Your assignment is to preach the gospel, everything else is secondary. Authentic fellowships are based on hearing the gospel from you, not how much they can get out of you!

One of the things I started during this year is not running my church into the ground. (Some choir members may disagree, but I still love them). The Lord has truly been gracious and has afforded me many opportunities to preach at other churches. However, I stopped asking the church to accompany me to every outside engagement. When our schedule is busy and I have multiple engagements I do not take the church everywhere I go. I always announce where I will be preaching in case someone wants to go, but it is not mandatory that they go and serve for every outing. I truly thank God for those troopers who never allow me to go by myself, but I do give them a choice to stay home and enjoy family time.

When I decide to not take the choir with me I inform the pastor who is inviting me that my church has been busy and if you want me to come I will be by myself. It's at that point you will discover if the invitation is about you preaching or filling the pews and offering plate. If the pastor chooses un-invite me I fully understand and do not carry any hard feelings, but I have to do what is best for the well-being my congregation. When your church family see that you care about their well-being and their time, when you do ask them to go with you they will be more likely to show up in great numbers. Never become a burden to your church trying to be a blessing to somebody else's church.

CUTTING BACK IS NOT A BAD THING

Years ago when a church was celebrating its anniversary or the pastor's anniversary it would be a week-long celebration. Kick-off one Sunday, have service all week and end on the following Sunday. Some churches still have services all week. There was a time when the church was packed every-night with members and visitors from the guest church. However, times have really changed. As I told you in the earlier chapters' people just do not come to church like they did before. In some cases we can barely get them to come consistently on a Sunday morning; and it's an even greater challenge getting them there during a week night. Therefore, for some churches to have services all week long may not be the best thing anymore; especially when it's the same 15 to 20 people showing up. When no one shows up to support the services it becomes more of a burden on the church than a blessing. Whether people show up or not expenses still has to be paid.

I know for some churches it is what you have always done, and it what the church is accustomed to, but "cutting back may not be a bad thing." To have a full week of services just because it's what has always been done, even though the people are not showing up is not a good practice. Maybe they are not showing up because they are tired and they have so much going on in their personal lives. Or could it be they are tired of hearing the same preachers for the last twenty years. Could it be they do not have the extra money and do not want to be embarrassed during offering time? With all the other things that are taking place at church, could it just be too much?

Furthermore, I know some churches look forward to these services because it's how they raise money during anniversaries; and cutting services mean cutting money. However, what should be considered when planning these services is that most of the times it's the same individuals doing all of the giving. If these services become a burden on them you may even lose your faithful supporters. When planning these services and anniversaries not only should we think about how the church will benefit, we must think about how taxing will it be on the people.

Therefore, if the way it was done in the past is not working and it has become overwhelming for the church and the members than consider cutting back. You still can celebrate the anniversaries just with fewer services. In some cases this has been found to be more fruitful financially and supportively. Every pastor has to do what works for his or her church, but we are living in a time when church attendance is not like was in the 80's & 90's. The worst thing we can do is invite a guest church to celebrate our anniversary and our members do not show up because they are tired from being in church all week.

Another thing to consider when it comes to anniversaries and week day/afternoon services is, are the preachers on the lineup ones that your congregation look forward to hearing. It is true that all members especially leaders should support the services regardless of who is preaching because it's their church. However, we should invite preachers who are going to meet their spiritual needs. If we do not take this into consideration members will show you how they feel about a preacher by not showing up. If it is a preacher they do not want to hear they will either give you multiple reasons why they cannot make it to service or simply not show up. On the other hand, if it is a preacher they want to hear, no matter what is going on they will press their way. This is one of the reasons why when inviting preachers we have to be prayerful and invite those who will take the assignment seriously and come prepared to feed the congregation the word of God.

DISCUSSION QUESTIONS

1) Have you noticed a change in attendance in afternoon/week day services? If so, what adjustments have you made or are planning to make?
2) What do you believe is the reason many people do not support services outside of Sunday morning?
3) Are all your fellowships fruitful and spiritually uplifting?
4) What is your position on annual dates?

Changing The Way We Minister To Youth & Young Adults

Changing the Way We Minister To Youth & Young Adults

"How can a young person stay on the path of purity? By living according to your word.

PSALM 119:9 NIV"

ONE OF THE CHALLENGES MANY churches are facing is the exodus of youth and young adults. The millennials (Born 1977 – 1994) are missing, and Generation Z's (1995-2012) are few in number. This has left many churches with only small children and babies, who really do not understand what is going on in worship. This is a serious concern because if our churches do not have active youth and young adults, who will lead our congregations in the future? The youth and young adults of today will be the leaders of tomorrow, but if they are not in church we will not have anyone to pass on the mantle of leadership. Therefore, we have to be strategic on how to get them back in church; but that is not it, we also have to minister to them when they get there.

A few years ago I began to notice that I did not have a lot of young adults in worship, and the few I had did not consistently attend. Initially, I tried to figure out why they did not come to church regularly, and why they were not involved in ministry. Then it dawned on me that maybe it is not anything wrong with them, but it is the church. By that I mean the church was not meeting their spiritual needs. We rarely used them in the worship service. There was no ministry taking place that was relevant to what they deal with on a regular basis. We no longer have a youth and young adult dance ministry or choir; everything is for the younger kids. If they did not usher, there was nothing else for them to do. All we offered was Sunday school and a morning sermon, but they can stay home and get that online. Many young people would rather stay home and watch worship on TV or online, especially if they feel the church is not relevant, or they are not getting anything out of the service.

This caused me to change my focus; instead of focusing on why they did not come to church I focused on making sure we have something to offer them when they do come. I have discovered that most people, especially young adults, go to churches that meet their spiritual and family needs; thus if I wanted to see youth and young adults in our church I had to make sure that we became a youth and young adult-friendly church.

WHY ARE SO MANY YOUTH AND YOUNG ADULTS LEAVING THE CHURCH?

Before giving my recommendations on how to become a youth and young adult friendly church, I have to deal with a bigger problem, and that is why they do not come to church. Have you ever wondered why youth and young adults do not come to church like we did when we were younger? (Well I'm still young at heart!) I asked a few of our members and some other young adults why so many in their generation do not attend church on a regular basis and these are some of the answers I received:

1) Too many church people are hypocritical, judgmental or insincere. One young person stated, "They tell us to come as we are, but they judge us when we come as we are."
2) They demonize everything we do as if they never did some of the same things. (This, of course, consists of their music, movies, culture and technology).
3) Church is boring! It is for children and old people. There is nothing for us to do.
4) The church makes us feel like we do not belong if we do not dress like them or act like them in church.
5) Church is not relevant! We don't talk about REAL stuff in most churches. We are judged if we talk about real issues such as sex, porn, masturbation, abortion, homosexuality, temptation and drugs.
6) I'd rather stay home and watch it on TV.
7) I have to work.
8) People are unfriendly and unwelcoming.

These were just a few answers I received, but I am sure there are many more. When I heard these answers it made me take a deeper look at our church to make sure we are not pushing them away from church, but that we are meeting their spiritual needs in addition to providing skills to deal with the challenges of everyday life. If you have not done so already, I recommend each church take a look at their Youth and Young Adult Ministry to ensure that it is relevant, and it deals with the "real stuff" that our young people deal with on daily basis.

RECOMMENDATIONS FOR CREATING A YOUTH AND YOUNG ADULT-FRIENDLY CHURCH

When creating a youth and young adult friendly church one must remember that both groups need a sense of belonging. They need to feel that this is their church not just a church they attend. They also need ministry opportunities that cater to their needs and meet them where they are. It is important to develop opportunities that will allow the youth and young adults to build healthy relationships in church. A few additional recommendations:

1) Give youth and young adults opportunities to serve and perform tasks that are valued within the worship experience other than youth day's and 5th Sundays. For example, allow them to read scripture, pray, work media, assist with offering, etc.

2) Look for opportunities to affirm them—send them the message that they are special and essential to the congregation. We often send a contrary message by ignoring young people, interacting with them only when we need to correct them. But for them to feel loved and appreciated, positive interactions need to far outnumber the negative. Spend time talking with them—give focused attention; if they are small children, get down on their level, eye-to-eye. Ask for their input and then use it.

3) Learn about their world. Get to know their concerns, culture, needs, preferences and challenges. Find out what they watch on-line, on television and in movies; what they listen to; what they read. How do you find out? Ask them! And then listen without criticizing. The point here is not for an adult to act like a teen (teens are turned off by that!)—rather, the point

is for the adult to understand the teen. A second part of this approach is to look for what is good and godly in the youth's world and then use that as a bridge to connect your world of Christ with what is consistent with Christ in their world.

4) Find ways to work together. Provide a church setting in which youth and young adults can gather to express and discuss their needs and fears.

PLAN OF ACTION FOR YOUTH AND YOUNG ADULT LEADERS

1) Youth leaders must identify what age group(s) are missing or inactive and begin to plan ministry to meet their needs.

2) Empower the youth/young adults that are present! Youth attract other youth and young adults.

3) Get to know them; learn their interests, needs, their gifts and talents, and find ways to incorporate ministry that encourages spiritual growth while adapting to a sinful world.

4) Find creative ways to get them to read and learn more about the bible.

5) Create a ministry where they can feel comfortable being who they are! Spiritual growth is a process.

6) Give them ministry responsibilities, and begin training them to become the leaders of the church.

7) Find ways to stay theologically sound, but become culturally relevant.

8) Teach them how to live out their Christian beliefs in a world with a "New Normal." The New Normal is the concept that anything goes and anything is acceptable.

9) Incorporate them in the worship experience as much as possible. Let them know they belong and are just as important as everyone else.

10) Be Relevant! One of the biggest mistakes churches/people make is substituting the true Word of God (Gospel) for the worldly entertainment in an attempt to attract young people into the church. We do not have to change the Gospel to make it relevant!!!!!!!!!

EVERYBODY CANNOT BE OVER YOUTH MINISTRY!

One of the mistakes many churches make is placing the wrong people over youth and young adult ministry. Just because someone has a child(ren) who is active in the youth or young adult ministry does not mean they qualify to be over the ministry. There is nothing wrong with parents assisting when help is needed, but leading is a different story. Too many parents have taken on the position just to provide opportunities for their child. Whoever is assigned to lead youth and young adult ministry must have a heart for all the youth and young adults. They must have a passion to make their lives better. There is a major difference between the sheer desire for a position in contrast to a heart for the ministry. We cannot have leaders who merely want the title, but do not want to do the work that comes with the title. This ministry requires a lot of time, sacrifices, compassion and creativity. Also, those who are serving on the youth and young adult ministry team must be able to relate to the generations which fall in that group.

Youth and Young adult ministry leaders must be spiritually grounded themselves before they can lead others; especially young people. They must be able to handle the truth, and the multitude of issues that our young people are facing in today's society. Youth and young adult leaders cannot be judgmental. While working with this age group you will encounter and hear many things that may be shocking. However, for many of our young people it is their reality; and if they cannot discuss them at church and find solutions what good is the ministry.

Furthermore, youth and young adult leaders must have a vision and mindset for ministry; if not it will turn out to be an extended "summer camp." By that I mean the ministry will only give trips and parties and fail to meet the spiritual and physical needs of the youth and young adults. I do believe that youth and young adult ministry should be fun and full of activities, but it must also provide a spiritual foundation and opportunities to deal with real life issues. Our young people need an outlet to have fun, but they also need solutions to deal with the challenges they face on daily basis. This is why those who are leading the ministry must be in touch with reality and be able to relate to the young people.

Finally, in my opinion every youth and young adult ministry team should have youth and young adults on the leadership team. Youth leadership opportunities are often overlooked by adults, either knowingly or unknowingly, but the results are the same; a lost opportunity for young people to take the lead. Young people are best poised to advocate for their needs in creating and implementing programs to ensure they are relevant and youth-friendly. They can relate to the youth in ways the adults cannot. Furthermore, youth involvement facilitates and develops future leaders. When you utilize youth in leadership roles, it ensures that the future generation is equipped with competencies necessary for strong leadership; it also enhances young people's understanding of how to be accountable and inspiring leaders.

Discussion Questions

1) Are the youth and young adults missing in your church? If so, what can be done to get them back?
2) How effective is your youth and young adult ministry? Is it meeting the needs of your young people?
3) Does the ministry deal with real issues that the young people are facing?
4) What can be done to get more youth and young adults involved?
5) Are the youth being trained and developed to become responsible leaders?

Changing Our Position: Getting Back On the Front Line

§

Changing Our Position: Getting Back On the Front Line

Learn to do right! Seek justice, encourage the oppressed. Defend the cause of the fatherless, plead the case of the widow.

— Isaiah 1:17

As a child growing up in Baltimore city, I remember when the churches lead the charge for community development. The pastors were visible in the community. They were the ones who challenged residents and city officials to keep our neighborhoods safe and clean. Whenever we needed something changed in our community the church was very instrumental in making things happen. As far back as I can remember, the church has always played an important role in the community, and in the lives of the people in my neighborhood. For example, when a tragedy happened in our neighborhood we went to the church to find peace and direction. When we were acting up at home or in school, our parents took us to talk with someone at the church. When we needed help with finding jobs or resources we went to the church for help. The church has always been the place where people went to have their spiritual, physical, and emotional needs met.

However, over the years something has drastically changed. In some communities the church is just a place where people meet on Sundays and Wednesdays for service, and take up their neighbors parking spaces. In some cities and areas the church no longer has a relationship with the residents in the community. It no longer serves as a voice and advocate for the people. Many church members and leaders drive into the community for worship and when church is over they leave the community until the following week. This lack of relationship and concern has caused a major disconnect between many churches and the communities in which they are located. As a result, some people in the community show no regard for the church, and many residents fight against the church. This is so unfortunate because the church and the residents should be working together for the betterment of that community. Also, the church is there to help the community and provide spiritual and physical resources, not be at war with the community.

I must admit all of the issues between churches and community is not because of the community, some churches have lost their way. Instead of being a place of empowerment for the community they have become just another building in the community. It is sad to say, but some pastors and churches do not even have a working relationship with their community. But if we are going to effectively fulfill the charge that God has given to the church we must get and back on the front line as advocates and leaders of our communities. This means we have to get out of our sanctuaries and go outside into the streets and build authentic relationships with the people who live in our communities. In addition, we have to advocate for the social, educational, and economic well-being of the people. The church must never forget that we have a Christian obligation to be an advocate and a source of strength for our communities.

WHAT IS THE CHURCH?

Before we can clearly understand the role of the church we have to understand the nature of the church. When most people hear the word church they probably think of a building with stained glass windows and a cross hanging on the inside. They automatically assume you are referring to a building. However, there are some people who may say that the church is not a building at all. For instance, the early Christian church had no buildings; they met in each other's homes. When the church grew they eventually began to meet in places of worship as we know them today, but when references were made about the church it mentioned people not buildings.

Therefore, we can agree that the church is not a building, but a collective body of believers with a specific purpose. It is comprised of those who have been saved and redeemed by the True and Living God, based upon the sacrifice of the Lord Jesus upon the cross. Inclusion in the Body of Christ is not by membership in a denomination, nor by baptism, nor or by dedication. It is not received by ritual, or by ceremony, or by natural birth. It is received by faith (Rom. 5:1; Eph. 2:8). The invisible church is the church made up of true believers. The visible church consists of those who say they are Christian, but may or may not be truly saved. Being a member of a church on earth, guarantees nothing. Being a member of the Body of Christ, guarantees salvation.

The word "church" comes from the Greek ekklesia which means "assembly" or "gathering." But, the church is more than a meeting place. It is much more than a gathering of believers who profess the true and living God and attend weekly worship meetings. The church is the bride of Christ. It is a living temple of the True God. The church is the totality of all true believers, regardless of denominational affiliation. The entire body of believers is the church, and as such, it is the dwelling place of the Holy and Infinite God.

THE PURPOSE AND FUNCTION OF THE CHURCH

The purpose of the church is to worship God, (Luke 4:8), study His Word (2 Tim. 2:15), pray (Acts 2:42), love one another (John 13:35), help each other (Gal. 6:2), partake of baptism and the Lord's supper (Luke 22:19-20), to learn how to live as godly people (Titus 2:11-12), and to be equipped to evangelize the world Matt. 28:18-20). Joseph Tkach says in his article, "Six Functions of the Church" that:

"Worship is God-centered and Christ-centered. It is not about entertaining Christians with flashy displays or presentations, but about expressing our love by worshiping our Creator. We are to praise and glorify God in worship. As such, every Christian needs to be part of regular fellowship and worship. Edification is also a role of the church. It involves edifying believers, but also nurturing, building up or helping believers to mature in Christ. To this end, churches are tasked with a variety of ministries such as Bible study, continuing education in related areas, praying for one another, acts of genuine hospitality and more. Evangelism is also a key role of the church. This means reaching out to a lost world with the Good News about Jesus. Since people often have questions or doubts about Christ and Christianity, knowing the truth and being able to defend it (apologetics) is also part of the role of the church. But beyond evangelism in the sense of reaching out with the gospel, the church must also express compassion and mercy tangibly by helping others. In following Christ's example to love others, the church, too, must seek to make a real difference in the world while not neglecting to share the message of Christ.

If a church fails to fulfill any of these key roles - worship, edification, and evangelism - then the church is not functioning as God intends. Granted, there are times when churches face challenges and struggles to one degree or another, but a healthy church seeks to overcome such challenges in a way that honors God and His intentions for His church. (Tkach, 3).

The book of James also gives some insight on the purposes of the church. James says "Religion that God our Father accepts as pure and faultless is this: to look after orphans and widows in their distress and to keep oneself from being polluted by the world." (James 1:27) The church is to be about helping those in need. Helping those in need means, in addition to preaching the Gospel, we should help with their physical and social needs.

SHOULD THE CHURCH GET INVOLVED WITH SOCIAL JUSTICE?

Recently I was asked the question if the church should get involved with social justice issues and my answer was absolutely yes! In the face of injustice and inequality the church should pursue justice and advocate for the marginalized. We should always be concerned about bringing light in the midst of darkness and equality for those who are being mistreated. Biblical mandates for justice abound in both the Old and New Testaments. Many of the biblical king's legacies were determined by how well they inspired, defended and promoted justice, as we see in Jeremiah 22:15-16. Prophets proclaimed and championed justice, while decrying Israel's current state of favoritism, oppression and moral depravity. Standing up for justice has always been a part of God's people. Jesus' ministry began with a declaration which pointed towards social justice:

"The Spirit of the Lord is upon me, for he has anointed me to bring Good News to the poor. He has sent me to proclaim that captives will be released, that the blind will see, that the oppressed will be set free, and that the time of the Lord's favor has come." Luke 4:18.

On numerous occasions Jesus acknowledged, and even identified Himself with the poor, outcast and marginalized. In Matthew's Gospel Jesus stated:

"Then the King will say to those on his right, 'Come, you who are blessed by my Father; take your inheritance, the kingdom prepared for you since the creation of the world. For I was hungry and you gave me something to eat, I was thirsty and you gave me something to drink, I was a stranger and you invited me in, I needed clothes and you clothed me, I was sick and you looked after me, I was in prison and you came to visit me. "Then the righteous will answer him, 'Lord, when did we see you hungry and feed you, or thirsty and give you something to drink? When did we see you a stranger and invite you in, or needing clothes and clothe you? When did we see you sick or in prison and go to visit you?

"The King will reply, 'Truly I tell you, whatever you did for one of the least of these brothers and sisters of mine, you did for me.'

Furthermore, all four gospels deal with freedom from oppression and poverty. The gospel of Jesus demands social responsibility and a response to injustice and oppression of God's people. The message of salvation is also a message of judgment against injustice, oppression, and is a condemnation of self-centeredness. Therefore, we must take the example of Jesus, speak truth to power and fight for justice for all.

As believers we must recognize that the world in which we live is filled with injustice and we must act. We must be willing to admit and address the complex realities within our world and communities. There's no way we can sit back and be silent when racism, classism, and now "Trumpism" are hurting our people. There is a clarion call for the church to stand up and get back on the front line and fight for justice of all people.

THE ROLE AND RESPONSIBILITY OF THE BLACK CHURCH

In the days of past, the clarion call and mission of the black church was two-fold: it served as a beacon of hope for the lostsoul seeking grace and mercy, but it also functioned as an oasis for all issues affecting the community. The black church served as a voice in the wilderness, crying out that equality and justice belonged to all persons, despite race, social status, or lived experience. The church operated as a twenty-four hour, full-service institution, affecting change spiritually, intellectually, emotionally, and socially. (Mattson)

In the Encyclopedia of African American Christian Heritage, Marvin Andrew McMickle wrote this insightful and informative article entitled: *The Black Church/A Brief History.* I thought it was important to include this entire article in this book because of the richness of its history:

During the decades of slacc very in America, slave associations were a constant source of concern to slave owners.
For many members of white society, Black religious meetings symbolized the ultimate threat to white existence.
Nevertheless, African slaves established and relied heavily
on their churches. Religion offered a means of catharsis...
Africans retained their faith in God and found refuge in their
churches. However, white society was not always willing to
accept the involvement of slaves in Christianity. As one slave
recounted "the white folks would come in when the colored
people would have prayer meeting, and whip every one of
them. Most of them thought that when colored people were
praying it was against them".

Religious exercises of slaves were closely watched to detect
plans for escape or insurrection. African-American churches
showed an air of militancy in the eyes of white Americans.
Insurrections such as Nat Turner's in Virginia, born out of
the religious inspiration of slaves, horrified white Americans.

Understanding the potential end which could result
from the religious experiences of African slaves, many white
Americans opposed the participation of Blacks in Christianity.

In African-American history, "the church" has long been
at the center of Black communities. It has established itself
as the greatest source for African American religious enrich-
ment and secular development.

This development is embodied in Christianity, and the
term, "the Black Church" presents many details of racial and
religious lifestyles unique to Black history. In essence, the
term "the Black Church" is a misnomer. It implies that all
Black churches share or have shared the same aspirations and

strategies for creating cohesive African-American communities. This is not true, and there were numerous differences found among Black communities which were reflected within their community churches. Black communities differed from region to region. They were divided along social lines, composed of persons from different economic levels, and maintained varying political philosophies. Black communities in the inner cities of the United States have traditionally differed from those in rural areas, etc.do you need the etc?? In The Negro Church in America, the sociologist E. Franklin Frazier noted, "Methodist and Baptist denominations were separate church organizations based upon distinctions of color and what were considered standards of civilized behavior."

Organized politically and spiritually, black churches were not only given to the teachings of Christianity, but they were faithfully relied upon to address the specific issues which affected their members. For many African-American Christians, regardless of their denominational differences, Black Churches have always represented their religion, community, and home. Scholars have repeatedly asserted that Black history and Black church history overlap enough to be virtually identical. One of the first known Black churches in America was created before the American Revolution, around 1758. Called the African Baptist or "Bluestone" Church, this house of worship was founded on the William Byrd plantation near the Bluestone River, in Mecklenburg, Virginia. Africans at the time believed that only adult baptism by total immersion was doctrinally correct.

Black people in America also supported the autonomy of their congregation to make decisions independent of a larger church body. Other early Black Church milestones included the Baptist and Episcopal denominations. The First African Baptist Church of Savannah, Georgia which began in 1777. This is said to be the oldest Black church in North America. Originally called the First Colored Church, the pastoral life of George Leile's preaching is tied to its beginning.

In 1787, Blacks in Philadelphia organized the Free African Society, the first organized Afro-American society, and Absalom Jones and Richard Allen were elected as overseers. They established contact and created relationships with similar Black groups in other cities. Five years later, the Society began to build a church, which was dedicated on July 17, 1794. The African Church applied for membership in the Episcopal Diocese of Pennsylvania. The end of the Confederacy signaled freedom for millions of southern black slaves and prompted the emancipation of the black church. This started the emergence of the black church as a separate institution.

At the time, white southerners still sought to maintain control over African Americans' worship, for both religious and social reasons. Such services typically emphasized the responsibility of the slave to be obedient and provided biblical justification for black bondage. Slaves had no voice in church affairs and were relegated to the rear of the church or the gallery, as spectators rather than full members of the congregation.

Post -Civil War: After emancipation, black churches became virtually the only place for African-Americans to find refuge. Blacks moved away from the "hush-harbors" that they retreated to for solace as slaves. Formally, during this time, a church separation petition was filed by thirty-eight black members of the predominantly white Fairfield Baptist Church in Northumberland County, Virginia, in 1867. Referring to the new political and social status of African Americans, the petitioners said they wanted to "place ourselves where we could best promote our mutual good" and suggested "a separate church organization" as the best possible way. A month later, the white members of the church unanimously acceded to the petitioners' request, setting the stage for the creation of the all-black Shiloh Baptist Church.

Once established, Black Churches spread rapidly throughout the South; the Baptist churches led in this proliferation. The 1800's ushered in many milestones that built on the foundation of the Black Church. To mention just a few, 1808 celebrated the founding of Abyssinian Baptist Church in New York City. Black Americans along with a group of Ethiopian merchants were unwilling to accept racially segregated seating of the First Baptist Church of New York City. They withdrew forever their membership and established themselves in a building on Anthony Street (later Worth Street) calling it the Abyssinian Baptist Church. The name was inspired by the nation from which the merchants of Ethiopia had come, Abyssinia.

Other new churches also emerged because of the missionary activities of black ministers. The Reverend Alexander Bettis, a former South Carolina slave, alone organized more than forty Baptist churches between 1865 and his death in 1895.

Services: With the division of congregations came the development of a distinct religious observance combining elements of African ritual, slave emotionalism, southern suffering, and individual eloquence. Working-class Baptist and Methodist church services fused African and European forms of religious expression to produce a unique version of worship that reflected the anguish, pain, and occasional elation of nineteenth-century black life in the United States.

Such services usually involved a devotional prayer provided by a leading member of the church, singing by the congregation and choir, and the minister's sermon. The prayer would request a powerful God to ease the earthly burden of the congregation and would be enhanced by the congregation's response, an expression of agreement with the words "Yes, Lord," "Have mercy, Lord," and "Amen."

After the prayer, the congregation typically showed their devotion through song. Even if a formal choir existed, all the members of the congregation would be expected to participate. Occasionally an individual member outside the choir would stand up and lead the house in song. By the turn of the century, most southern black church choirs had assumed the responsibility for presenting the hymns, but the "call and response" tradition continues today.

The third element in a classic black service was the minister's sermon. Building on the long tradition of slave preachers and "exhorters," many ministers employed all the drama and poetry at their command, injecting vivid imagery and analogy into their biblical accounts conveying understanding of the rewards of righteousness and the wages of sin. Not every minister was capable of eliciting such a response. But those ministers who did avoid "emotion without substance" and stirred their congregations to strive for a more profound faith and more righteous way of living in a world of adversity provided spiritual guidance for a people whose faith and capacity for forgiveness was tested daily. For these people the black church was indeed "a rock in a weary land."

Nineteenth-century black churches ministered to the needs of the soul and served a host of secular functions, which placed them squarely in the center of black social life. Church buildings doubled as community meeting centers and schools until permanent structures could be built, and during Reconstruction they served as political halls. The black church provided shelter for visitors as well as temporary community theaters and concert halls where religious and secular plays and programs were presented.

In a blurring of spiritual and social functions, church members provided care for the sick or incapacitated and financial assistance to students bound for college. They also sponsored virtually all the many fraternal lodges that emerged in the nineteenth-century South. As racially-motivated violence and terrorism ran rampant across the country, Black churches were staunch in their resistance.

In 1886 blacks organized the National Baptist Convention, in a continued attempt to reduce the influence of white national bodies among blacks. As the number of Baptist churches grew, they met regularly in regional conventions that then evolved into statewide and national organizations. By 1895 the various Baptist associations had formed the National Baptist Convention of America, representing 3 million African American Baptists, primarily in the South.

The African Methodist Episcopal (AME) Church emerged as the second-largest, post- Civil War black denomination.

Because of its independence, the AME Church had always been viewed with suspicion in the antebellum South, having been forced out of South Carolina following the Denmark Vesey conspiracy of 1822. The church was reorganized in South Carolina in 1865 by Bishop Daniel Payne and grew to forty-four thousand members by 1877. Similar growth in other southern states gave the AME Church, by 1880, a national membership of four hundred thousand. Its followers were, for the first time, concentrated in the South.

Other denominations completed the spectrum of black church organization in the South. The Colored Methodist Episcopal (now Christian Methodist Episcopal) Church, which grew from the black parishioners who withdrew in 1866 from the predominantly white Methodist Episcopal Church, and the African Methodist Episcopal Zion Church each claimed two hundred thousand members by 1880.

In 1895, a meeting attended by more than 2000 clergy was held in Atlanta, Georgia. The three largest conventions of the day: the Baptist Foreign Missionary Convention, the American National Baptist Convention and the National Baptist Educational Convention merged to form the National Baptist Convention of the United States of America. This brought both northern and southern black Baptist churches together. Among the delegates was Rev. A.D. Williams, pastor of the Ebenezer Baptist Church and grandfather of the Rev. Martin Luther King, Jr.

However, the more involved Black Churches became in sparring against the racial intolerance and violence targeted against them, the more the churches and their members were punished. Within the church, the Presbyterians and

Episcopalians also saw the division of their memberships into white and black denominations, with each of the two black churches having some one hundred thousand members by 1900.

In 1908, The Christian Index published the "Colored Methodist Bishops' Appeal to White America-1908." In their statement, church leaders responded to the surge of mob violence and lynching occurring across the country, denouncing terrorism waged against Black persons and imploring the country to suppress the spread of anti-Black violence. As anti-Black terrorism proliferated into the twentieth century, Black churches grew increasingly vehement in their calls for castigation of racial violence. Also on September 15, 1915, the National Baptist Convention of America was formed.

Between World War I and World War II, the black church continued to be not only an arena of social and political life for the leaders of blacks; it had a political meaning for the masses. Although they were denied the right to vote in the American community, within their churches, especially the Methodist Churches, they could vote and engage in electing their officers. The election of bishops and other officers and representatives to conventions has been a serious activity for the masses of blacks.

Almost a century ago, the Black church was an organizational site for social and political activities, centers for economic development and growth. As microcosms of the larger society, Black churches provided an environment free of oppression and racism for African-Americans. In black churches, African-Americans were consistently exposed to social, political, and economic opportunities which could be sought and had by all members equally. The representational structure of African-American churches confirmed Black preachers as both religious and community leaders. The sermons of many Black preachers expounded messages of Christianity analogized to the daily experiences of African-Americans. Thematic expressions of overcoming oppression and "lifting while climbing," were first articulated in church sermons.

Civil Right Era: During the Civil Rights era, Black churches were well established social and political power bases for African-Americans. Their enormous presence naturally, sanctioned them with the political power to lead Black people in the movement for civil rights. Some churches and their organizations were completely opposed to any involvement in the political struggle for civil rights. Others chose to participate and did so passionately, organizing by rallies, protests, and marches, while teaching Christianity and community involvement.

In the late 1940's, 50's, and 60's, the Black Church functioned as the institutional center for Black mobilization. They provided an organizational base and meeting place for African-Americans to strategize their moves in the ongoing fight against racial segregation and oppression. As Black Churches became the epicenter of the social and political struggles for Black equality, they increasingly became targets for racially motivated violence. An extensive assault on members of a Black community took place by burning a Black Church.

The bombing and burning of Black churches during this time translated into an attack upon the core of civil rights activism, as well as upon the larger Black religious community. The most infamous example of racist American church destruction occurred on September 15, 1963. When the Sixteenth Street Baptist Church in Birmingham, Alabama was fire bombed, the explosion was felt by the entire Black community. Four children were killed in the attack, several others injured, and a community's sense of security within their church was forever traumatized.

This act signified the depths to which racial hatred could fall. Like many other churches bombed before and after, the Sixteenth Street Baptist Church was a Black Church. Even though the Ku Klux Klan (KKK) was implicated in this crime, members of the KKK were not the only ones responsible for similar acts of terror throughout the country. Unfortunately, this was not an isolated incident. These racially motivated arsons did not destroy the souls of Black communities. In 1988, the National Missionary Baptist Convention of America was formed.

In the 1990 C. Eric Lincoln book, " The Black Church in the African American Experience" with Lawrence H. Mamiya, they described the, "seven major historic black denominations: the African Methodist Episcopal (AME) Church; the African Methodist Episcopal Zion (AMEZ) Church; the Christian Methodist Episcopal (CME) Church; the National Baptist Convention, USA., Incorporated (NBC); the National Baptist Convention of America, Unincorporated (NBCA); the Progressive National Baptist Convention (PNBC); and the Church of God in Christ (COGIC)," as comprising "The Black Church."

In the twenty-first century, the Convention movement of the African American Baptist Church has undergone several changes. The individual organizations remain important to African American religious life. The Black Church is also at a crossroads due to 'White Flight," gentrification and systemic capitalism. The Black Church has historically been a source of hope and strength for the African American community.

If change and justice is going to take place in our communities, the church, especially the "black church" must get back on the front line and be the beacon of hope. It has always been a part of our history and in this 21st century the need is even greater. As long as there is unequal pay based on gender and race, racism and racial profiling, mistreatment of people of color, the marginalized, open season on black males, and underperforming school districts, just to name a few, there will always be a need for the Black Church to be on the front line. Let's not ignore the struggles of our people while we sit in our sanctuaries having worship; it's time to change our positions and let our voices be heard until we see positive results.

DISCUSSION QUESTIONS:

1) How involved is your church in Social Justice and community affairs?
2) Do you know the major needs of your community?
3) Would the residents in your community consider your church to be a community- friendly congregation, or an advocate for them?
4) What programs does your church offer to help with the issues your community is facing?

CHAPTER NINE

Changing The Way We Serve God's People

Changing The Way We Serve God's People

Share with God's people who are in need. Practice hospitality.

- Romans 12:13

But everything should be done in a fitting and orderly way.

- I Corinthians 14:40

BEFORE I STARTED MY PASTORAL journey at the New Hope Christian Baptist church, I served as the youth pastor at the New Bethlehem Baptist Church in Baltimore, Md. under my pastor Dr. Anthony M. Chandler Sr. During that time, as his youth pastor, I learned many lessons that have shaped my pastoral leadership. Dr. Chandler was a stickler for time, everything must start on time. He was also a pastor who cared about people; hospitality was very important to him and his ministry. The lesson that stuck with me the most was his passion for excellence. He taught us that "everything must be done with a spirit of excellence." The motto for the New Bethlehem church was to become a "5 Star church," and everything we did he demanded that we do it with a spirit of excellence. I remember it like it was yesterday, he told me that we serve an excellent God and everything we do for God must be done in excellence.

When I was called to pastor my first church, I carried that same mentality with me and I tried to set a standard of excellence in that congregation. When I became the pastor of my current church (Holy Trinity Baptist Church) I did the same thing and set a standard of excellence in this congregation. The challenge is that some people may not understand my passion and desire for achieving excellence and it may come off as me being too demanding. However, in order to achieve excellence we have to sweat the small stuff, because everything matters. During my first few months as pastor, I constantly talked and taught what it takes for us to become that 5 Star Church. Some members caught the vision and ran with it right away, while others, you know how it is, they gave some resistance. One of the lessons I learned from my pastor is that you do not waste time trying to change people, you change the environment, and people will adjust to the environment or go somewhere that they are comfortable!

The first thing we did in striving to become a 5 star church was started working on our appearance. We raised money and renovated our sanctuary. This project was more than just renovating the sanctuary; it was the beginning of our transformation. After making those renovations to the upstairs it ignited a fire in our members, which has not gone out yet. We have been working and restoring our entire church ever since. It was at this point that small things started to matter and everyone began paying attention to things they may have overlooked before. Sometimes all it takes is a pair of fresh eyes and a vision to begin the transformation process.

Some people may not agree with this statement, but presentation makes a difference in a church. A clean and beautiful sanctuary makes the church more inviting to visitors. On the flip side, a dirty sanctuary that's falling part can turn some people off. It is hard to get comfortable in unclean places. No one wants to visit a dirty hotel or restaurant; and they should never have to visit a dirty church. God's house should always be ready to receive worshippers. This means we have to teach our members to reverence God's house, especially the sanctuary. It is so unfortunate that some people treat God's house like they treat their own house, not like it's a sacred place of worship. I'm not suggesting that we have to worship the sanctuary; it's just a building. However, we should treat it with reverence. It's the place where we have corporate worship and invite God's presence to show up.

I remember when I was young we could not chew gum or eat anything in the sanctuary, but times have really changed. I have seen people eating in the sanctuary like they were in the school cafeteria, and then leave the trash in the seat or on the floor. These days, people do and say any and everything in the sanctuary. Often times we have to remind people that they are in the sanctuary and not on the playground. There must be some reverence and respect for God's house, and the sanctuary. I am sure someone reading this book will ask why? Why must we respect or show reverence for a building or a room? Here is why?

In the book of Exodus, God declared that the sanctuary is the place where He will dwell. "And let them make Me a sanctuary; that I may dwell among them." Exodus 25:8.

In 2 Chronicles 7:15-16, God says, "Mine eyes shall be open, and mine ears attentive unto the prayer that is made in this place. For now have I chosen and sanctified this house, that my name may be there forever: and mine eyes and mine heart shall be there perpetually." When God declared that He would be attentive to prayers made in "this place," He was not referring to just one specific location. That promise applies wherever the people of God gather to worship Him. Webster's dictionary also offers a religious definition: "a house consecrated to the worship of God; a place where divine service is performed." The definition goes on to refer to the Old Testament, where the word sanctuary indicates "the most sacred part of the Tabernacle, called the Holy of Holies, in which the Ark of the Covenant was kept, and into which no person was allowed to enter, except the High Priest, and that was only once a year to intercede for the people."

However, we cannot assume that everyone knows what to do and how to do it, therefore, we have to teach our members how and why we should honor God's house. We should all have a class on church etiquette. Some may not think it is important, but etiquette in the church shows a reverence for God's presence. It shows a concern for the feelings and well-being of fellow-believers, and others who are in attendance. As believers, we should always honor God's house. Food or beverages should never be brought into the sanctuary and should only be used in the places designated, as a way to honor God. We should treat God's property with respect. Do not write in the song books or use them to dispose of gum. The song book racks are not to be used to dispose of trash. Children should never be allowed to play in the sanctuary or with the microphones and instruments.

In addition, we should teach everyone to honor the worship services. This means being on time and ready to worship. Come not just for service, but expecting to have a personal encounter with God. This may seem a little over the top, but remember God will honor those who honor Him. Therefore, let us always seek the honor that comes from above by practicing proper church etiquette and reverence for God's house.

Becoming a Multicultural Church

Have you ever sat in church and wondered where did everybody go? Have you ever wondered what happened to the members? There was a time when the church was packed and it was hard to find a seat, but on some Sundays you can sit wherever you want. What's going on with the church? This is a question many pastors and congregants are asking all across this country; churches are not full like they were years ago.

As I mentioned in one of the earlier chapters, there are many reasons why many churches are experiencing a decrease in membership, but one of the main issues our churches are facing is that our communities have changed. Members have retired and relocated, the children have grown up and have gone off to college, or gotten married and moved with their spouse. Due to high property taxes many people have decided to move to an area which is more affordable. All communities are changing because people are leaving. However, not only are people leaving the community, people of different races and cultures are moving in. Many inner city communities are becoming more diverse than they have ever been. There is nothing wrong with a diverse community, the challenge becomes when the religious institutions are not equipped to handle or minister to a diverse community.

Therefore, the problem is that our communities have changed, but our churches have not made the necessary adjustments; therefore we are unable to fully minister to those in our immediate communities. In order to meet the needs of the communities in which our churches reside we must become more multicultural. Here is why; when the congregation is not prepared for diversity they may become culturally insensitive. This type of attitude will make visitors feel uncomfortable and it will drive them toward the door as fast as they come in.

Stereotypical imagery is a problem; so are the distant looks that say go away instead of a welcoming smile with words of affirmation. If there is a general impression that people other than "us" are not accepted here, people will not stay. When individuals of a different ethnicity or background come in they must be greeted not only by the official greeters, but by the congregation at large. Everyone should be treated fairly and made to feel that they belong. Some churches should invest in an interpreter to reach deaf and Spanish speaking families. This will expand the ability to meet the needs of the community at large.

WE KNOW IT'S A NEED SO HOW DO WE GET STARTED

The first thing the church should do is get to know the people in the community. Secondly, identify and try to meet some of their needs in order to demonstrate the love of God in their everyday lives. This begins to build bridges, showing the community that the church really does care. Churches grow through community service.

We must also create an environment that makes it ok to be different. The church must learn how to celebrate and respect differences. Remember everyone does not worship the same, neither do they understand all of what's being done in the worship service. Therefore, always be understanding and let people know its ok to ask questions. Be flexible and willing to do some things differently to meet the needs of everyone. Becoming a multicultural church will not happen overnight, however it's time to start preparing now because our communities and churches are changing. We have to be ready to minister to whomever God sends through those doors, even if they don't look or speak like us.

SERVING THE COMMUNITY
Jeremiah 29:7 says, "Seek the peace and prosperity of the city to which I have carried you into exile. Pray to the Lord for it, because if it prospers, you too will prosper." Just as bridges and cities go together, churches and communities are linked. God's people are to be connected to the city, the community, and the world.

If the church is going to effectively serve the community we must build healthy relationships. In addition to building relationships with residents, we must also build relationships with elected city officials. We may not agree with every policy decision made by our city leaders, but it is still important to find common ground to create effective partnerships. Partnerships will benefit churches and communities, especially when both sides are working together on behalf of the people. Plus, city agencies can help churches develop a needs-assessment that identifies what your city/community needs and how you can be part of the solution.

Moreover, if we are going to serve the community we must be present and visible in the community whenever we can. Pastors and churches must let the city know that they want to be partners in any appropriate situation. If your community sponsors a holiday parade, enter a float every year. If they need a place to host a civic event that doesn't contradict your core values, make your space available. Give back to the community as often as you can. Take advantage of every opportunity to show how much you love the community, without expecting anything in return.

This means being a blessing to those in need. The job of helping the less fortunate really doesn't belong to politicians or civic leaders. From God's perspective, His people need to be leading the way in helping those who are hurting (Matthew 25:31–46; Luke 4:16–21). Whether it's hosting the homeless on a cold, winter night or volunteering for after-school mentoring programs, believers can show God's love in a lot of different ways; we just have to be willing to do it. The church will be stronger and more effective when it becomes a community-oriented church. So get out there and be a blessing and watch God bless your church in return!

Discussion Questions

1) Do we operate with a spirit of excellence? What can we do better when it comes to hospitality?
2) How can we improve the way we serve visitors?
3) How can we improve the way we serve the community?
4) Are we a multicultural church? If not, what steps do we need to take to become a church for all?

CHAPTER TEN

Ready For Change!

Ready For Change

IN THE BEGINNING OF THIS book I made the statement that the church is in trouble. I stated that it was a code red because something drastic is happening to the church. The thing that is drastic is the church is drifting into a dangerous place and some people do not even realize it; they're still shouting and having church. Everything is changing and many churches are not what they used to be, but the problem is that they have not noticed the shift. If that's not the case, they have ignored the shift and continued to function as they have always done in the past. There comes a time when all churches have to make some adjustments so that we can stay relevant to the times in which we live. The challenges for many churches is the members would rather have a museum instead of a fruitful ministry. Unfortunately, many of our churches have become museums.

How can you tell if your church is a museum or a ministry? Here are a few clear ways to tell whether your church is a museum or a ministry. Museums celebrate the past; ministries operate in the present. Museums keep everything; ministries give things away. Museums design their buildings to house artifacts; ministries design their buildings to equip disciples. Museums have plaques on items dedicated or donated to the organization; ministries dedicate all their resources to the glory of God. Museums attract one-time visitors; ministries keep people coming back. Here is the million dollar question; Has your church become a museum or is it a disciple-making ministry?

Many churches have become museums because they refuse to change anything. Just because God never changes doesn't mean your church shouldn't. In fact, the most effective churches change constantly. Effective churches never change the mission or the message (those are eternal). But they always change the methods to make sure the mission stays alive and the message gets heard.

If change is going to take place in the church it starts with the leadership. The leaders must understand that it's their job to take people from where they are to where they need to be. Change has to be taught and carefully planted in the minds and hearts of the people. If not, you will face major resistance.

In the book Drive: *The Surprising Truth About What Motivates Us*, Daniel Pink talks about the importance of influencing the employee's motivation to change. The premise being, that in order to successfully change an organization, the change needs to well up from within the ranks of the employees – and in the church this includes members and volunteers. Figuring out what motivates people to change is key, and there needs to be targeted efforts to identify the heart of what motivates them.

SUCCESSFULLY MAKING CHANGES TO YOUR CHURCH WITHOUT DESTROYING IT

One of the things that has helped me implement change is helping people understand the change. Change is scary when it is not understand. Make every effort to ensure members understand the what and why, so they are not preoccupied with mental "what ifs" of the change. Consider how the change will impact the entire church. For successful change to occur there needs to be a target. Write measurable goals so you can assess whether the change had the intended result and impact on the organization. If you can't measure it, you can't manage it. Take the time to create the necessary systems and processes to ensure a smooth transition. Also, make sure any needed resources are available. For instance, if a new ministry is created in response to member needs, make sure there is adequate funding and staff and/or volunteer support.

Moreover, having the right leaders in place is vital. Change efforts succeed or fail based on the effectiveness of the leadership. Identify someone who has the passion, motivation and talent to lead the change. Then let them run with it. Implementing a change quickly can be a scary thing, but the faster you can get through it the quicker the organization will get back in the rhythm of ministry. Churches often drop the ball on communicating information that people need to help them understand. Take the time to think through the questions your members might have and answer questions before they are asked. This will take the unknown out of the equation and will help to control the rumor mill.

Finally, implementing any kind of change requires systems and processes. Make sure your change effort has the necessary support to ensure a smooth transition. Taking the time to plan every specific detail of a change and developing a strong communication plan to help engage members and volunteers in the process is the best way to turn your church around quickly and successfully. Ready for Change? Great! "Let's Go and Change The Way We Do Church!!!!!!!!!!!!!!!!!!!!!!!!"

BIBLIOGRAPHY

§

Moss-Kanter, Rosabeth, *Ten Reasons People Resist Change*, Harvard Business Review. 9/25/12.

ARTICLES

Johnston, Ted, *How to Make Your Congregation Youth-Friendly*, 2015.

Tkach, Joseph, *Six functions of The Church*, 2016.

Tinson, Nicole, The Role of The Black Church in Creating Change, 2013.

Robert S. Harvey, *Restoring the Social Justice Identity of the Black Church*, 2010, Vol. 2 No. 02.

Mattson, Stephen, *Social Justice is a Christian Tradition-Not A Liberal Agenda*, 2015.

REFERENCE:

The Center for African American Ministries and Black Church Studies 5460 South University Avenue Chicago, IL 60615, V: 773-947-6300. *An Encyclopedia of African American Christian Heritage* by Marvin Andrew McMickle, Judson Press, Copyright 2002. ISBN 0-817014-02-0

Barna, George, *The Habits of Highly Effective Churches*, Regal Books, Ventura, CA. 1999.

Pink, Daniel, Drive: *The Surprising Truth About What Motivates Us*, Riverhead Books, NY. 1995

Stetzer, ED; Dobson, Mike, *Comeback Churches*. B & H Publishing, Nashville, TN. 2007.

Swindoll, Charles R. *The Church Awakening: An Urgent Call To Renewal*, Faith Works, New York, NY. 2010.

Toler, Stan; Nelson, Alan, *The Five Star Church: Serving God's People With Excellence*, Regal Books, Ventura, CA. 1999.

Schnase, Robert, *Five Practices of Fruitful Congregations*, Abingdon Press, Nasbville, TN. 2007.

Made in the USA
Middletown, DE
15 June 2017